HOW TO BE A MINISTER

How to be a Minister

———

GERALD KAUFMAN

faber and faber

LONDON · BOSTON

First published in 1980
by Sidgwick and Jackson Limited
This edition first published in 1997
by Faber and Faber Limited
3 Queen Square London WC1N 3AU

Phototypeset by Intype London Ltd

Printed in England by Clays Ltd, St Ives plc

A CIP record for this book
is available from the British Library

ISBN 0-571-19080-4

2 4 6 8 10 9 7 5 3 1

To my constituents in
MANCHESTER
who made these experiences
– and this book –
possible

Contents

———

Acknowledgements

———

Lord Wilson of Rievaulx and Lord Callaghan of Cardiff, the two Prime Ministers in whose administrations I served, both read the first edition of *How to be a Minister* in typescript. Harold Wilson sent me a list of observations and corrections, meticulously set out in his small, clear handwriting. James Callaghan wrote me a detailed letter, again containing helpful comments and suggestions. I was grateful to both of them for their interest and generosity. Neither, of course, was in any way responsible for the views I express in this book, or for any errors of fact in it; vanity, however, compels me to quote from James Callaghan's letter: 'I have now completed reading your MS and found it a real pleasure. Indeed I enjoyed parts of it so much that I think you lulled my critical faculties! . . . I regard it as a monument of good advice to any aspiring minister and it should be read by all of them.'

Lord Varley, Secretary of State throughout the time I held office at the Department of Industry and an old friend, read my original text of *How to be a Minister* chapter by chapter as I was producing it, and cast a benevolent eye over this revised version. I thank him for his encouragement as well as for his tuition in ministerial crafts during my four years at his department; he too bears no responsibility for my reflections on those experiences.

I offer my thanks, too, to the office of the Secretary of the Cabinet and to the staff of the House of Commons Library for their unflinching answers to a volley of apparently irrational and even absurd queries that I put to them in my efforts to bring this new edition up to date. All accuracies are owed to them; all inaccuracies are my own.

It will quickly become apparent that throughout this book I refer to the putative Minister to whom I seek to give instruction as 'he' although, of course, there will – or should – be at least as many women as men who both wish and ought to become Ministers. To have resorted throughout to 'he or she' would have been found infelicitous, I hope even by most anti-sexist readers. So, lazily, I have fallen back on the generic 'he'.

It might be asked, very fairly, why I did not employ the generic 'she'. I could respond that there are, at present, more men than women Ministers, more men than women MPs and more men than women Parliamentary candidates. Such an excuse would sound probably opportunistic and certainly unconvincing.

So let me recall a conversation I once had with the Right Hon. Denis W. Healey. I asked Healey how it had come about that the 'W' in his name stood for Winston. He explained that he had been born during the First World War; that his father had much admired Winston Churchill, who had been First Lord of the Admiralty; and that accordingly Healey senior had, as a gesture of admiration, given his baby son the additional Christian name of Winston.

I asked Healey why, if his father had admired Churchill so much, he had not given his son Winston as his first, or indeed only, Christian name. Healey replied, 'Hell, a gesture's a gesture.'

Now Read On . . .

———

Governments change (sometimes, or, at any rate, sometime). Prime Ministers prosper and then pass. Policies are propagated, practised, pilloried, and then purged. New departments are created, old ones are discarded, divided, merged. Ministries and their ministers move into brand-new or renovated buildings. Yet through political change, renewal and decay, the essence of government remains unaltered.

It is more than seventeen years since I last set foot in a government department as of right, as a Minister of the Crown. Yet, when I have subsequently visited departments either to argue a case for ministerial action or as a guest of the minister, I have found things pretty much the same as when I left the Department of Industry for the last time in April 1979.

The Department of Health may have moved into a building which resembles an ossified blancmange. It may have been presided over by a hyperactive chatelaine who hustled belatedly into her room for a scheduled meeting ('I am afraid Mrs Bottomley is behind schedule again', murmured a member of her Private Office staff, resignedly), who conducted a discussion while moving around the room at a run, and who left abruptly, almost in mid-sentence, for another engagement. This dynamic lady may have been succeeded by Stephen Dorrell, placid almost to the point of torpor. Yet the routine for being received by both of them remained reassuringly the same: the messenger escorting me to the waiting room, polite yet vigilant to ensure that I did not stray into forbidden inner purlieus; the Secretary of State's Private Office, with staff telephoning away; the government-issue sofas and armchairs; the beverage, served in government-issue crockery, unable, quite, to make up its mind whether to be tea or coffee; the officials, middle aged, armed with bulky briefs, clearly extremely competent, and equally clearly set in their ways.

The Department of National Heritage has been housed in premises, off Trafalgar Square, so glitzy as to make Planet Hollywood seem faded and drab. Yet the Whitehall machine has taken it over and, relentlessly, re-fashioned this unlikely and incongruous home in its own familiar yet determined image.

Downing Street has been turned into a fortress, with huge, guarded gates erected either to protect Prime Ministers from the people or the people from Prime Ministers. Once the gates have been penetrated, the front door has been opened, and one has passed through that old familiar corridor, little has changed. Guests arriving for a state dinner are still, as they were a generation ago, presented with a table plan on which their own place is indicated by an accusatory finger. There are still drinks in one of the state rooms, a receiving line in an adjoining room, further drinks in yet another room, and then a languid saunter into the large state dining room, where seatings have been calculated with a meticulous instinct for the precisely appropriate hierarchical order. Even the food seems the same.

Prime Ministers' styles, of course, vary. In the study where I had once worked with Harold Wilson, I was received by Margaret Thatcher, a Joan Crawford who believed herself to be Anna Neagle or else an Anna Neagle maligned as Mommie Dearest. I suggested to her that, if the National Enterprise Board were still in active existence, it could have provided finance to keep going an electronics factory in my constituency that was faced with closure. The Prime Minister turned to the relevant junior minister, Kenneth Baker, who was there to back her up and to brief her. 'What did I do with the National Enterprise Board, Kenneth?' she asked, at a momentary loss, as if she had mislaid some item of bijouterie. And when, forlorn at a response from her which I regarded as negative, I said that more than two hundred employees would shortly lose their jobs, she responded, grandly, 'I want jobs for all my workers.'

Downing Street accepted and absorbed that style. Just as equably, it went on to accommodate the ameliorative approach of John Major, a man so pleasant that, only a short while after I had pilloried him as The Man Who Came to Dither, he could make a special point, at a state dinner, of leading me across to Hosni

Mubarak and informing the President of Egypt, 'I am sure you will enjoy talking to Mr Kaufman. He knows a great deal about the Middle East.'

The government machine has coped with Thatcher and Major, with Bottomley and Dorrell. The Treasury has ingested and expectorated Norman Lamont, who became a hero of Gorton Labour Club when he rejected the advice of his officials and over-ruled a damaging VAT decision made against the club by the Chairman of Customs and Excise himself. The Department of the Environment has said goodbye and then hello again to Michael Heseltine who, minutes after being savaged by me in a House of Commons debate on local government finance, met me behind the Speaker's Chair, listened to my plea on behalf of an urban regeneration project in my constituency, and gave speedy instructions that the scheme should go ahead.

The Ministry of Defence has said hail and farewell to Sir John Nott. Nott, adamant in upholding a veto on a Royal Marine constituent of mine being allowed to attend a memorial service in Derby for his Marine cousin, killed in the Falklands, suddenly found it possible for my constituent to go to Derby after all; I having pointed out to the Secretary of State on the telephone how such a story would look on the front page of the *Daily Mirror.*

The Home Office has mourned the loss of William Whitelaw who, sitting next to me in a make-up room at Border Television's studio in Carlisle, bristlingly assured me that, whatever the Peacock inquiry into broadcasting might recommend, advertising would appear on the BBC only over his dead body.

The Home Office has survived Leon Brittan, who niggled away at proposals regarding the amount and percentage threshold of the parliamentary deposit that, as Shadow Home Secretary, I put to him as conditions for Labour facilitating the passage through the Commons of a Representation of the People Bill. Agreement was reached only when the government Chief Whip, John Wakeham, lying on a couch and listening in despair to our sterile interchange, begged Brittan to accept the deal.

In a variety of departments, Whitehall has adored Douglas Hurd as one of its own. As Home Secretary, he reversed a deportation order on an Asian in my constituency after I took the man's threatened family to see him at the House of Commons and their toddler tottered about the room, playing with ministerial impedimenta. When Hurd was Foreign Secretary, I, once again his Shadow, conspired with him in his vast and cavernous office on King Charles Street to do down opponents of firm action by the United Nations against Saddam Hussein. He showed me his – a government motion seeking approval for all necessary measures to free Kuwait – and I showed him mine – a Labour amendment which gave a very slightly different slant to the identical objective. I then assured him that Labour would support his motion and he counterassured me that the government would accept my amendment. What did *you* do in the Gulf War?

The Lord Chancellor's Department has profited from the tenure of Lord Mackay of Clashfern. After a stalling action lasting months by that department over an alleged miscarriage of justice that a constituent of mine complained he had suffered, Lord Mackay welcomed me into his room in the House of Lords, sat me down, and, before I could utter a word, told me that my constituent's case had been handled deplorably and that compensation would be paid to him.

The old Department of Employment got more than it bargained for from Lord Young as Secretary of State. I went to see him to plead for Leon Bosch, categorized (under apartheid) as a South African 'Cape coloured'. A star double bass player at the Royal Northern College of Music in Manchester, Bosch had been offered a job with an orchestra in Britain, but had been refused an employment permit and would therefore have to return to South Africa, where orchestral jobs for Cape-coloured double bass players were thin on the ground. When, at our meeting, Lord Young's officials warned that to give Bosch a permit would create a dangerous precedent, I asked how many South African Cape-coloured double bass players there were studying in Britain. As Young escorted me to the lift I asked him, as one Jew to another, to think of Bosch as another Jew. Young told me it would be all right; it was; and Bosch went on to achieve a splendid career in Britain as a double bass virtuoso.

And the government machine coped with me as a back-bencher in the 1992 Parliament. I ran totally amok in pursuing a campaign of refusal to have anything to do with a man called Michael Bichard. Bichard, Chief Executive of the Benefits Agency, persisted in dealing with my constituents' social security cases after I had made clear that I disapproved of the newly created Next Steps Agencies (of which the Benefits Agency was one) and insisted that parliamentary accountability could only be fulfilled if the Secretary of State himself responded to my correspondence. Though I raised the matter at Commons question time, in parliamentary debates and in newspaper articles, Bichard just went on writing to me, even when I returned his letters as unwanted to the Secretary of State. At a loss as to what to do next, I rang up the office of the Chairman of the Post Office and asked his assistance in defending me from receipt of unsolicited mail; the Post Office explained that, unless correspondence was obscene, it was their statutory duty to deliver it to the addressee. I next telephoned the office of the Chief Constable of West Yorkshire – the headquarters of the Benefits Agency being located in Leeds – and reported to him an alleged criminal offence, namely the insistence of an individual in sending me letters even though I had made clear that I did not wish to receive them. The officer who took my call asked me the name of the alleged offender, and I explained it was the Chief Executive of the Benefits Agency. There was a pause and then the voice at the other end of the telephone said, soothingly, 'I do understand, Sir'; but went on to explain that there was no prima facie evidence of a crime. Reports of these extraordinary, not to say demented, manoeuvrings got back to the Secretary of State's office and the Whitehall machine decided to paint round me, accommodating what it regarded as my eccentricity without ever acknowledging that it was doing so.

Not simply because it bent to what it saw as a whim and I asserted as a principle, the Whitehall machine in this instance – as in hundreds of others, large and small, of which I knew – demonstrated its majestic imperturbability. It bends not because it must but because it decides that to do so is the politic course. The power of that machine, I knew from experience both in and out of office, could support ministers, could frustrate ministers, could absorb ministers. The original edition of this book, in 1980, was intended as a primer for politicians, an effort to explain how to live with the machine and, if need be, how to defeat it.

As the years went by after its publication, I was told by the Secretary of the Cabinet that *How to be a Minister* was recommended to incoming ministers in the Conservative government.

Ministers thanked me for it, even asked me to autograph their copies. Kenneth Clarke, as Chancellor of the Exchequer, told the Treasury and Civil Service Select Committee of the House of Commons in 1993, 'There is one book I recommend to all my colleagues upon first taking office, written by Gerald Kaufman, called *How to be a Minister*. It remains the best guide.' I began to wonder if I carried some exiguous moiety of guilt for the continuance of the Tories in office.

Kent Durr, the last South African Ambassador in London prior to Nelson Mandela becoming his country's first black President, told me that, as a Minister in his country's unreformed government, he had read and profited from *How to be a Minister*. I asked myself whether I was burdened with a minor role in the continuance of apartheid or, on the contrary, could claim some minute credit for the end of apartheid.

It seemed to me, seventeen years after its original publication, that the book might deserve another outing. I therefore set to work to revise it and, where appropriate, bring it up to date. Yet, although it now includes examples and experiences from the 1980s and the 1990s, the story it tells still begins as long ago as June 1970. So: now read on . . .

Prologue

———

I arrived at Number Ten at about 11 a.m. It was 19 June 1970. Labour had unexpectedly lost the General Election. A few hours before, in Manchester Town Hall, the Returning Officer had declared me duly elected as Labour Member of Parliament for Ardwick. Driven by a good friend from the Labour Party in Manchester, John Williams, and accompanied by another friend, the comedian Harry Fowler, who had spoken at my eve-of-poll meeting and stayed to help on polling day, I had then gone across to Huyton to join Harold Wilson, for whom I had worked for the previous five years as Political Press Adviser. But the counting of the votes in Manchester had taken much longer than expected and Wilson, anxious to get back to London and pack his bags at Number Ten, had been unable to wait. Only a handful of his dejected constituency supporters remained at Huyton Labour Club clearing up the debris of defeat. A nightmare journey followed. The car, as if unable to bear our political tribulations, repeatedly broke down; we lost our way and at one point – driving, remember, from Liverpool to London – we found ourselves in *Worcestershire*! By the time we discovered the right road the sun had come up to begin a perfect, cloudless June day, the first day of the new Tory government. More and more miserable, listening on the car radio to the toll of Labour defeats, and having dropped Harry off in Chelsea, we arrived in Downing Street.

We parked the car at the House of Commons – the first use I had made of my brand new status as a Member of Parliament – and I went into Number Ten to help pack. A pall of bereavement hung over the place. As the day wore on, the Prime Minister left for the Palace to resign. The new Prime Minister, Edward Heath, moved into the official areas of the building on the ground floor. In the private apartments on the second floor we toiled away in a room which had once been my office – a room where much of the planning for the Prime Minister's election campaign had taken place – like survivors on a tiny desert island whose beaches were awash with the rising high tide of Toryism. Late that night we finished. We left by the back door of the building, walked across the garden where a few weeks before Harold Wilson had confidently given the television interviews announcing his dissolution of Parliament, and went out into Horseguards Parade. Before the gate finally thudded behind us I looked up at Number Ten for the last time and, unforgettably, saw silhouetted against the window of the Cabinet Room the figure of Edward Heath consulting with the very same civil servants who earlier that day had still been advising Harold Wilson. We all occasionally make petty, semi-superstitious little gestures; and at that moment I vowed to myself that I would not set foot again in Downing Street until Harold Wilson was back in Number Ten as Prime Minister.

On the morning of Monday, 4 March 1974, I called into the Leader of the Opposition's Room at the House of Commons. In the general election the previous Thursday the Conservative government had lost its majority and, with five fewer seats than Labour, was not even the largest party in the Commons any more. Edward Heath had spent the weekend trying to work out an arrangement with the Liberals that would keep his administration in office. During the 1970–4 Parliament it had been suggested to me that I should return to Harold Wilson's staff as his Parliamentary Private Secretary; but, while flattered and honoured, I felt that I should work to find a role for myself as a back-bencher. I had, though, remained on close terms with Harold Wilson and his family, and with his personal secretary, my very good friend Marcia Williams. So it was as a friend dropping in that I knocked at the door.

I had spent my own weekend recovering happily (with an increased majority) from my constituency election campaign. The winter weather during the election had been cruel; I was still recuperating from frost-bite; I was exhausted; and I paid only limited attention to reports of the comings and goings in Downing Street. So I was surprised, when I arrived at Harold Wilson's room, to find it buzzing with lively purposeful activity. The news was that Heath had failed in his negotiations, that he would very likely be resigning later that day, and that Harold Wilson was expecting to be called to the Palace to form a government. I was irresistibly (and unresistingly) caught up with the preparations, and before long found myself lunching in a private room at the St Ermins Hotel with Harold Wilson, Marcia Williams, Joe Haines, Harold Wilson's Press Secretary in Government and Opposition, and a new member of his staff, the academic Bernard Donoughue, who had joined him to help in the February election. From there we went on to the Wilsons' Westminster house at 5 Lord North Street. The afternoon wore on and then, suddenly the call came. Harold Wilson was asked to go to the Palace. Two of the old familiar Rovers from Number Ten came round to collect his party. And to my astonishment I was asked to join it.

We all drove into the courtyard fronting the Palace façade, and then through an archway into a rear courtyard. Harold Wilson went into the Palace. The rest of us waited in the cars. After a few minutes he came out again, as Prime Minister. And then, for me a crowning moment of my life, we drove to Number Ten. Harold Wilson was back, and my superstitious boycott was over. We went inside, and the new Prime Minister began forming his government. Edward Short (Leader of the House) had got there before us. Others followed: Eric Varley (Secretary of State for Energy), Roy Mason (Defence) and, among others, George Thomas. George, an old and good-humouredly voluble friend, had been Secretary of State for Wales in the previous Labour government, and arrived confident that he would be asked to go back to his old job. He was bitterly chagrined when he learned that he was being asked not to join the government at all, but instead to take on the non-party post of Chairman of Ways and Means (Deputy Speaker of the House of Commons). Within a couple of years George was to reach the acme of his political life as Speaker of the House. But that March evening at Number Ten he taught me a useful political lesson. If the Prime Minister makes you an offer and you are not in an exceptionally powerful position, take what you are offered or be ready to return to the back benches; dozens will be ready to accept what you have rejected. In the middle of the evening Harold Wilson took a break to go into the Press Room and watch the television news of his return to office. I sat there, alone with him, and together we gazed at the filmed re-enactment of the scenes we had participated in a few hours before. In the dusk, with the look on his face of a dazzled schoolboy who had unexpectedly been given a fantastic treat, Harold Wilson turned to me and murmured: 'I still can't believe it.'

Three days later I was back at Number Ten, and a few days after that back at the Palace for an audience with the Queen as a new member of her government. When I had returned with Harold Wilson to Downing Street it did not even occur to me that he might ask me to join his administration. I had vaguely wondered, earlier in the day, whether I might be invited to become his Parliamentary Private Secretary, and if so I was not sure whether I would accept. But later on, a friend by then in the Cabinet told me that the Prime Minister might offer me a job as an Under-Secretary of State. On the morning of Thursday, 7 March, my telephone rang and a Downing Street Private Secretary said that the Prime Minister would like to see me. I walked into the Cabinet Room – and our relationship had changed completely. I was now a very new, very inexperienced, very junior colleague, and a great distance opened up between myself and my old friend, now my awesomely remote boss. Very rightly, he allowed me no greater familiarity with him than any other junior minister. And very rightly he made me a very junior minister indeed, one of a large number who manned the huge Department of the Environment. At the time, though I readily accepted the post, I was not sure that I liked being at the very foot of the tree. But in requiring me to learn the job from the bottom Harold Wilson did me an inestimable kindness. He helped me to acquire the most precious commodity for anyone who holds ministerial office: experience. I did all the most menial jobs, and I gained from doing them.

Fifteen months later I was transferred, still as an Under-Secretary of State, to the Department of Industry. The Common Market referendum had taken place in June 1975. Much to Harold Wilson's irritation I had voted against the government's recommendation that Britain should remain a member of the European Economic Community. Now, in the post-referendum reshuffle, I was moved away from a Secretary of State, Anthony Crosland, whom I liked and admired and from a department whose work fascinated me, to an alien and novel field; I could not help feeling that it was some kind of punishment for misbehaviour. But six months later I was promoted to the rank of Minister of State, and given such assignments as representing the United Kingdom government at the hearings in Washington on the application for Concorde to land in the United States, and steering through the Commons the Bill nationalizing the aircraft and shipbuilding industries. I remained at the Department of Industry until the Labour government resigned on 4 May 1979.

I have not written this book because I believe I was any better a minister than all my able colleagues in that Labour government. But I have seen politics from vantage points that few others have enjoyed: ten years as a political journalist, working often at Westminster; five years on the Prime Minister's staff at Downing Street; five years in government, including two months with the Contingencies Unit at the Cabinet Office, a quite unique assignment given to me by James Callaghan during the strikes of early 1979; and – heaven help me! – twenty-two years on the Opposition benches, including twelve years as an elected member of the Shadow Cabinet and five years as Chairman of a House of Commons Select Committee. During my period as a minister I had the opportunity of carrying out large chunks of the Labour Party's election manifesto. I also learned quite a lot about how British government works. My aim in this book is to try to communicate something of what I have learned.

1

How to Become a Minister

———

Before you begin the process of learning how to be a minister, you first have to become one. An obligatory first step is to become a Member of Parliament or – in the case of the Conservative Party, even preferably – a peer. How to accomplish this is the subject for a separate treatise, possibly from the pen of a Dostoievsky.

Election to Parliament achieved, it is generally necessary for the party to which you belong to have won the preceding general election. This, however, is not absolutely essential. Sir William Jowitt was appointed Attorney-General in the Labour government of 1929 after having been elected to Parliament as Liberal MP for Preston a week before in that year's general election. After inclusion in the government he then, very sensibly if succumbing somewhat to conformism, joined the Labour Party. Sir William's subsequent career demonstrated a similar capacity for grasping opportunities as they presented themselves. When the Prime Minister, Ramsay MacDonald, split the Labour Party in 1931 and formed a national government, Jowitt followed his patron into the newly formed National Labour Party, and retained his ministerial portfolio. In 1935 he was defeated after transferring to the somewhat esoteric constituency of Combined English Universities, but re-emerged victor at a by-election in Ashton-under-Lyne in 1939 as a member once more of the genuine Labour Party, in nice time to be available for office in the war-time coalition government, in which he served with alacrity as Minister of National Insurance. When Labour won in 1945 he was the natural choice as Lord Chancellor, a position he retained throughout the six years of that administration. He was a member of all four of the different governments which ruled Britain between 1929 and 1951 and, as one observer acutely commented, was 'fortunate that his honest changes of political principle coincided so conveniently with the opportunities for holding office'.

A more recent example of supple political flexibility was the case of Reginald Prentice, who resigned from the Labour government in 1969 in protest at its inadequate concern for overseas development almost simultaneously with his removal from the post of Minister of Overseas Development. In Opposition he obtained a place on the Shadow Cabinet in 1972 as a result of Tribune Group support bestowed in return for his anti-Common Market views, became in the subsequent Labour government Secretary of State for Education with responsibility for introducing legislation imposing comprehensive education on all local authorities, appeared on pro-Common Market platforms during the 1975 referendum and then, having run the four-minute mile along the road to Damascus, in 1979 turned up in a Conservative government which slashed expenditure on overseas development and repealed the comprehensive education legislation that he had introduced.

Most politicians, however, will be elected to Parliament as a member of one particular political party and, rather unoriginally, perhaps, remain a member of that same party. Generally – though not always, for some of the most attractive politicians are genuinely unambitious even though they sometimes obtain office – they will hope at least mildly to obtain advancement within that party. For them the first and most important rule is: be noticed. There are some MPs who go through a long and hard-working parliamentary career without the leader of their party being very sure who they are. One Labour member, with more than a generation of constructive activity on the back benches behind him, told me that, though they sat in Parliament together for more than ten years, Clement Attlee never once acknowledged him when they met (even though, when he was once ill in hospital, he received a very nice note with a signature which he could not decipher but which, upon investigation, turned out to be that of his leader).

If Roy Jenkins had ever formed a government it would, if based on the Prime Minister's personal acquaintance with his ministers, have had to be unusually compact, since he very rarely spoke to anyone whom he did not know well, and this group was severely limited in size. During the leadership election of 1976 John Morris, a senior Labour minister whose views very closely resembled those of Roy Jenkins, told me that he would vote for Jenkins provided that before the close of poll the candidate said 'Good evening' to him in the Division Lobby; his vote was cast for someone else. On occasion this failure to make contact is the fault of the party leader. Sometimes, however, it is because of the inability of the aspirant minister to make sufficient of a mark.

This must be remedied; but not, however, by being too notice-able. Rowdiness in the House, being named by the Speaker, perpetual rebellion, may all gain headlines and even lead to popu-larity in one's constituency. They are not, however, a certain guarantee of office. That does not necessarily mean that you should become a total sycophant. True, some Prime Ministers warm to the genuine and dedicated sycophant. When Edward Heath was Prime Minister he could scarcely get through a question time without being assailed with devotion by the likes of Cranley Onslow and Norman St John-Stevas. Witnessing these events from the Oppo-sition benches one felt that the display was so obvious and so glutinous that it would fail if only through overkill. But no, both were rewarded with junior office. Genuine loyalty, as distinct from the characteristics of a political chameleon, is, however, a rightly valued quality which is properly rewarded.

Some Prime Ministers do indeed seek to create an administration consisting entirely of political clones of themselves. In addition, though, Prime Ministers face the need to provide representation for the various ideological strands in their parties, partly in order to achieve an equitable balance, partly to keep certain troublesome nuisances quiet. Anyone who wishes to qualify for the latter cate-gory should manage a nice compromise between being troublesome enough but not too troublesome. Voting against the government on a confidence motion or personally insulting the Prime Minister is not recommended. Paul Rose, an able Labour Member of Parlia-ment, was bewildered and hurt at being omitted from Harold Wilson's 1974 administration but discerned no link between this circumstance and a letter he had written to the *Guardian* some time before calling for Harold Wilson's resignation as party leader on grounds which doubtless seemed compelling at the time. On the other hand Eric Varley and Gwyneth Dunwoody both inadvertently got it absolutely right when, without being ostentatious about it, they defied a three-line Whip and voted against the Labour govern-ment's application in 1967 to join the Common Market. At the time Eric Varley was gravely advised by the Chief Whip, John Silkin, that if he proceeded on this hazardous path he would forfeit all hope of ministerial office. To some extent directly because of this warning he persisted, only to find himself within months a Whip serving under that same Chief Whip, whom he eventually preceded into the Cabinet.

The Labour Party is full of groups, of which that with the politically highest profile is the Tribune Group. These days the Tribune Group is so all-inclusive that a Labour MP, whatever his position in the party spectrum ranging from left to right, has to make a determined effort to exclude himself from Tribune, which has become so all-embracing that the only disqualification from it is to be a Conservative (and, indeed, members of the Campaign Group, a defiantly left-wing body, might claim that under New Labour being a Conservative could be a positive qualification for being a Tribunite). During the period when a substantial left wing existed within the Parliamentary Labour Party, there was always a place in a Labour government for the less turbulent members of the Tribune Group, to join which, indeed, was felt to give members a chance of preferment regarded as unfair by those MPs who shared many of the Tribune attitudes but did not believe in joining groups or even forming them. Sometimes, even the more boisterous Tribune groupies were recruited to office but, finding after a time that their position on the front bench inhibited them from asking the Prime Minister critical supplementary questions, resigned on genuine principle and spent much of the remainder of their careers writing articles denouncing – sometimes validly – what they saw as the insidious influence of the civil service.

However disappointingly such appointments may turn out – from the point of view of either the donor or the recipient – they are at any rate accepted (though by some reluctantly) as the prerogative of the Prime Minister. No Prime Minister likes to have his appointments selected for him by the press, and particularly not by aspirants to office who have the ear of the press. An exceptionally talented Labour MP, the late John Mackintosh, never received the recognition he might have expected, partly because in his earliest days in Parliament he sought so strenuously to receive it, constantly peregrinating upwards to the Press Gallery premises situated vengefully in some of the less attractive attics of the Palace of Westminster. Another Labour MP was constantly telling sympathetic journalists of his desire to become Minister of the Arts but never attained the post though he was ideally suited to it. A malicious rumour was spread that he had spent the eve of poll of one general election witnessing a Wagner dress rehearsal at Covent Garden, but the MP concerned vehemently denied this as a calumny. He eventually left the Labour Party and joined the Social Democrats, thus demonstrating conclusively his lack of desire for government office.

Ability, then, is not necessarily its own reward; but it certainly helps. It pays to be able to speak well in the House, though if this were the sole qualification Mrs Thatcher's government would have been denuded; her Minister of State at the Department of Industry, no Demosthenes in any circumstances, once made a speech so abysmal that, while his own back-benchers sat sunk in silent despair, Labour members waved their Order Papers in genuine appreciation. It pays also to achieve a reputation for having a competent grasp of a subject. Reg Freeson, who knew more about housing legislation than any civil servant in the Department of the Environment, was an obvious choice as Minister for Housing. Denis Howell, an ex-referee, was an equally inevitable Minister of Sport. During the 1966 Labour government Joel Barnett, Edmund Dell and Robert Sheldon marauded impressively from the Labour back benches on economic and financial subjects and were requited in the 1974 government by being selected as, for a time, practically the entire Treasury team under Denis Healey. Later in that administration one Labour MP made an intolerable nuisance of himself on a sensitive industrial topic but, in doing so, impressed the Prime Minister, James Callaghan, with his ability to such an extent that he would certainly have been promoted had the Labour government survived. However, the subject on which expertise is demonstrated has to be of reasonably general interest: the persistent advocacy by the Labour MP Gwilym Roberts of the manufacture of artefacts designed for the use of left-handed people never brought him the recognition that sinistralists were sure he deserved.

Over-exposure at Question Time is not recommended; it can lead to a reputation for frivolity, particularly if accompanied by stunts. Stunts themselves can be fatal. The appearance one day in the Chamber of the Conservative MP John Wells ostentatiously eating an apple (which turned out to be perfectly within the rules of order) aroused pleasure among his orchard-owning Kent constituents but provoked frowns on his front bench. Similarly, the presence one Budget Day on the Conservative benches in Mao uniforms of two MPs, Hugh Dykes and Robert Adley, both recently returned from a trip to China, did not prevent – indeed may have caused – their both being passed over in Margaret Thatcher's administrations, even though at any rate one of them had discernible ability.

Work in a committee can help, whether it be a Standing Committee of the House considering an item of legislation, a Select Committee performing a semi-inquisitorial role, or a back-bench committee of one's own party. In the Parliamentary Labour Party a special forum is the Party Meeting. There are regular weekly Meetings, and also occasional Meetings called to discuss special topics, all open to every Labour MP. Some members address these Meetings frequently, and are accepted either with affection or irritation as party 'characters'. One member in the recent past raised with unfailing regularity topics relating to the Common Market, while another for a time attempted to persuade his colleagues to intervene with the BBC in order to achieve fairer reporting of some recondite subject, dear to his own heart, on the radio programme 'Today in Parliament'. Eric Heffer always spoke so quietly that, as soon as he opened his mouth, there were cries for him to speak up. It was suspected that he did this quite deliberately, in order to gain attention; if so, the ruse never failed. The speakers who attract the greatest attention at Party Meetings are those who attend reasonably often but speak only occasionally, though with knowledge and authority: MPs always respect someone who has done his homework. It is serious activity of this kind which gets a member talked about approvingly by his colleagues, such talk inevitably reaching the leader through the acknowledged conduit of his parliamentary Private Secretary. The party leader always makes a point of attending Party Meeting, but naturally is not involved in the work of the various committees.

Being Parliamentary Private Secretary to the leader, whether in government or Opposition, is itself almost a guarantee of office. Among Cabinet ministers who achieved success by this route were Anthony Barber, James Prior, Eric Varley and Peter Shore. Envious colleagues felt that the only clue to the otherwise puzzling appointments of John Stanley and Adam Butler to the relatively senior positions of Minister of State in Margaret Thatcher's May 1979 government was that they had both served her in Opposition as PPSs. The one glaring exception to this rule was Timothy Kitson, who soldiered on as PPS to the Prime Minister throughout Edward Heath's tenancy at Downing Street, earning at the end the tepid consolation of a knighthood together with, sadly, the torrid disdain of Margaret Thatcher for anyone who refused to pretend that Edward Heath was a figment of the historian's imagination. Patronage by some other senior minister can be almost equally powerful: if Roy Jenkins had not rescued Reginald Prentice from dismissal in Harold Wilson's 1975 reshuffle, the Labour Party would have been saved a great deal of subsequent trouble.

Membership of the Shadow Cabinet (in the Labour Party elected by one's fellow MPs, in the Conservatives appointed by the leader) is a certain guarantee of high office if your party wins the next election. Activity in one's party organization outside Parliament can also help. Members of the National Executive Committee of the Labour Party have a better than sporting chance of appointment, not only because they can be relied upon to voice the aspirations of the rank and file but also because the Prime Minister, relying on the doctrine of collective ministerial responsibility, can hope – sometimes, alas, forlornly – to secure a vote in favour of government policies at National Executive meetings. Office in the Conservative Party can similarly bring its reward; occupancy of deputy chairmanships boosted the careers under Margaret Thatcher of James Prior and Angus Maude, and a vice-chairmanship did wonders for the previously obscure prospects of Reginald Eyre. It is, however, a paradox that appointment to government office can positively damage the prospects of election to the Labour NEC – as Stanley Orme rose ever higher in the Labour government, his vote for the NEC increasingly wilted – while resignation from the government helps measurably: Eric Heffer never looked back as an NEC candidate from the day Harold Wilson sacked him from the Labour government for rebelling on the Common Market. In the Conservative Party, on the other hand, noisy exhibitionism from a minister safely in government is a positive recommendation for party office, whether achieved (Quintin Hogg) or constantly anticipated (Michael Heseltine).

Being Welsh or Scots is also a help in the Conservative Party, because of the need to fill numerous positions at the Welsh and Scottish Offices. It does no harm in the Labour Party either, but Labour has so many Scots and Welsh MPs that they have to take their chance with the rest, though naturally receiving preference for the Welsh and Scottish Office posts; at the latter department Judith Hart received her first Ministerial opportunity, her representation of the Lanark constituency overriding her birth in Burnley. (Nor was being a woman a disadvantage to Judith Hart, since both Harold Wilson and James Callaghan deliberately gave opportunities to women while, surprisingly or perhaps not so surprisingly, Margaret Thatcher did not.) The Conservatives, though, have so few Scottish and Welsh MPs that manning the Scottish and Welsh Offices is a constant headache to Tory Prime Ministers. In 1979 the Conservatives were thrown into consternation when their Shadow Scottish Secretary lost his seat in Glasgow. In 1970 Edward Heath was at such a loss to find an appropriate nominee as Secretary of State for Wales that he finally – either ingeniously or despairingly – lit upon Peter Thomas who, while representing the decidedly un-Cymric constituency of Hendon South, at any rate had the right kind of surname and antecedents. Subsequent Conservative Prime Ministers, increasingly desperate, appointed Secretaries of State for Wales of entirely English origin, offering the excuse that their constituencies (Worcester in the case of Peter Walker) were in reasonable proximity to the Principality. John Major eventually gave up even this pretext, appointing an MP from Yorkshire who some suspected had never even set foot in Wales, the only perceived rationale behind this appointment being that the Welsh and Yorkshire accents were equally incomprehensible to Major.

Being a barrister, and preferably a QC, also helps, since every Prime Minister has to find suitable candidates for Lord Chancellor and for four English and Scottish law officers. This requirement accounts for some unusual appointments: as Attorney-General in 1929 of Sir William Jowitt (for details *vide supra*) and as Solicitor-General – a post which, confusingly, cannot be held by a solicitor – of Sir Frank Soskice immediately upon his first election to Parliament in 1945 and of Sir Ian Percival, whose advancement on any other grounds would clearly have been preposterous, in 1979.

If, for whatever reason, Downing Street one day telephones and announces that the Prime Minister would like either to see you or speak to you, either seize the opportunity firmly, or reject it and do not afterwards complain. John Cronin in 1964 turned down the opportunity of becoming Parliamentary Secretary at the Ministry of Aviation, on the perfectly understandable ground that he felt he deserved something better, and never murmured afterwards at being passed over. Elystan Morgan nearly rejected an appointment by mistake. Tracked down by the police while touring his vast Cardigan constituency during one of Harold Wilson's more abrupt reshuffles, he somehow got it into his head that the person at the other end of the telephone offering him the post of Under-Secretary of State at the Home Office was not the Prime Minister but Jeremy Thorpe doing one of his accomplished impersonations; happily, the matter was sorted out speedily. Another candidate for appointment, upon receiving an offer from his leader, replied that he would like to think it over and was accommodatingly informed that he could have thirty seconds; he accepted. Conversely, Douglas Jay, after being dismissed by Harold Wilson, telephoned the Prime Minister next day and told him that, having slept on it, he would after all like to remain in office.

Above all – and this may be thought painless advice coming from someone who was lucky to be appointed to government office early in his parliamentary career – if you never get an offer at all, do not grow bitter. One Labour MP, who lurked for nearly thirty years on the back benches, was confident that he, rather than the upstarts who actually held these positions, should have been either Foreign Secretary or Chancellor of the Exchequer, and became so objectionable that his constituency finally got rid of him. On the other hand, Maurice Edelman, who was as able as, if not more so than, most of his Labour colleagues who sat in Parliament during his own thirty-one-year incumbency, accepted the position gracefully, looked after his constituents with great care, performed other political duties with grace and distinction, and wrote books of admirable quality. Being a Member of Parliament is in itself an honourable position, which thousands covet and never attain.

But, if you do get the offer from Number Ten, grasp it and make the most of it. That is what the rest of this book is about.

2

Two Dangerous Diseases

You have been appointed. For the first time, you walk into the government department to which you have been assigned. You are, understandably, highly pleased with yourself. And at that very moment, with your defences down, there on the threshold will await you the bacilli of two potentially debilitating diseases. If you do not very rapidly develop immunities to cocoon yourself in a protective skin, you are defeated before you have even begun. The diseases to which you are in imminent danger of falling prey are ministerialitis and departmentalitis.

The most immediately observable symptom of ministerialitis is a perceptible swelling of the head. Ministerialitis may be defined as a preoccupation and satisfaction with holding ministerial office to the exclusion of almost all other considerations. Of course as a new minister you should want to do a good job, for your own self-respect and for the good of your government and your party. But you should never forget that there is another world out there, a world that includes Parliament, your party, your constituency and, though sometimes you may be tempted to forget it, a whole country going about its daily business and rarely sparing you a thought unless you do something that particularly annoys it.

The problem is that once you walk into that department it is so easy to forget all those considerations. You enter a world that, unless you are determined to break free of it, seals you in as securely and hermetically as if you were in a space capsule hurtling in orbit miles up in the sky. To begin with, you will almost certainly have arrived not on foot but by car: what is more, by chauffeur-driven car (though the word 'chauffeur' is never employed in the Government Car Service, 'driver' being preferred). All ministers, at whatever level, have access to a car which collects them from home in the morning and returns them at night, picks them up from the station when they arrive from their constituencies, takes them to and from their official appointments and to and from Parliament, and transports them on various other journeys specified in rules laid down by the Prime Minister. Use of an official car is prohibited for all activities relating to party politics or constituency work. When I visited the ICL factory in my constituency on ministerial business, I was transported in a government Wolseley driven by a green-uniformed lady driver; when I went as the local Member of Parliament, I arrived in a friend's Mini.

If you remain a minister for very long you may forget entirely what it is like to travel on the public transport system to which those you represent are consigned. Your access to the car will be the more assured, the more elevated your status in the administration. But the most junior minister, even if not provided with his own personal driver, can generally at least get a car from the GCS pool. All ministers' cars are now fitted with cellular telephones, a levelling measure which has put an end to the élitist days when some privileged cars were equipped with radio telephones, which seldom worked properly but gave the driver tremendous status among his colleagues.

When you, the minister, walk through the door of your department, doormen will salute you. There will often be a special lift for exclusive use by yourself and your colleagues, a few of the more senior civil servants, and distinguished visitors. You will have a private entrance to your own office, sometimes a private washroom. Messengers will hasten to do your bidding, to bring you tea or coffee, to serve you drinks. All the daily newspapers will be provided for you together with the political weeklies and any other publications your fancy takes; one Labour minister boosted the circulation of a recondite publication named *Red Mole* by at any rate one copy during his tenure of office. Curiously, it is difficult to lay on anything much in the way of food; when I worked through lunch time at the office, I was generally sustained by a tinned salmon sandwich and an apple brought by my driver from a neighbouring sandwich bar. The sandwich was brought to me in a paper package but could just as easily have been delivered in a ministerial red box which, embossed in gold with a crown, the royal insignia and the minister's official title, follows him around from office to home like a faithful dog.

You will have at least one buzzer on your desk which, when pressed, will bring in a Private Secretary to cater to your demands. These, if you are extravagantly minded, can include the complete redecoration and refurnishing of your ministerial office. This facility was offered to me when I joined the government, and I was visited one day by a pair of artistically minded officials, complete with pattern books, who were much downcast when I told them that all I wanted was the repainting of a wall which had been left particularly grubby by my Conservative predecessor. No such commonplace inheritance awaited Reginald Freeson, the Minister for Housing, who took over from Paul Channon in 1974 an office which looked as if it were the product of a demented interior decorator suffering from particularly disturbing hallucinations. For a time visitors were ceremonially shown round it, evoking the slightly terrified awe customarily aroused by the wilder extravagances of Mad King Ludwig of Bavaria. The unbelievably expensive wallpaper gave the impression that meetings on such sober subjects as municipalization or rent control were being held in a Jacques Cousteau bathysphere. Meetings were, indeed, something of an ordeal, since the furniture included chairs which resembled purple kidneys, on which it was physically impossible either to sit or even to lie down. Eventually they were removed.

Any minister, however junior, can summon any civil servant in his own department, however senior. Meetings with other ministers are a different matter. There is a strict pecking order. An Under-Secretary of State will be 'on call' (ministerialitis, like all medical conditions, is subject to its own special clinical jargon) to a Minister of State or his equivalent, who in his turn will be on call to a Secretary of State. At the Department of the Environment Reginald Freeson, my senior as a minister, and Anthony Crosland, the Secretary of State, both generous and thoughtful comrades entirely lacking in any manifestation of conscious superiority, never once entered my Under-Secretary of State's room; I do not think Anthony Crosland even knew where it was. When ministers of different departments but of the same rank need to meet inter-departmentally (as distinct from Cabinet meetings, which are held at 10 Downing Street, or Cabinet Committees, which generally meet at the Cabinet Office at 70 Whitehall) the encounter takes place at the department whose Secretary of State is higher in order in the list of Cabinet ministers issued by the Prime Minister's office.

Even a junior minister has the authority of the whole government behind him, and can expect that the most senior industrialists or businessmen will respond to a request to call upon him. Such persons will indeed sit quite meekly while being lectured or hectored, and will arrive at inconvenient hours or days (Saturday morning, for example, was the time at which I once summoned a meeting of industrialists, plus the inevitable Lord Goodman, when vainly attempting to save a television tube factory from closure), and will often respond readily or even enthusiastically to requests which might superficially appear outrageous. British ambassadors home for briefings will call to be told the latest departmental line; foreign ambassadors will ask permission to pay their respects, often bringing with them letters from counterpart ministers written on heavy, crisp paper in incomprehensible languages, or even small gifts.

Gifts can indeed be an embarrassment, since there are rightly very strict limits on what a minister may be permitted to accept. Anything of appreciable value has either to be rejected, returned, handed over to the department or, if the minister takes a particular fancy to it, paid for. One Conservative minister, whose wife was brought by an Oriental potentate a watch which she could understandably not bear to part with, had to cough up several hundred pounds so that she could keep it. Fortunately, any gifts I received were curiosities of little intrinsic value, though one at any rate caused a scare. I was told one day that a very suspicious-looking package had arrived for me, origin unknown. It was brought in and certainly looked ominous, large in size, rectangular in shape, and with strange knobbly protuberances. The necessary security procedures were invoked and, after a nervous interval, we were assured that the object was not malignant. My Private Secretary, with great courage, opened it to reveal a hard covered folder, decorated in patterns doubtless of a symbolic character, and studded with small, definitely non-precious stones. It was a thoughtful gift from one of Europe's less celebrated republics, and has come in useful as a cover in which to keep *Radio Times*. Nevertheless, it was definitely a gift, and in its own small way a contributor to ministerialitis.

Anything which cossets you or makes you feel special contributes to ministerialitis. There is one police area in England which arouses dormant symptoms by insisting on providing ministerial visitors with a Special Branch escort. Once, when I opened a Christmas Fayre, a uniformed constable was assigned to protect me (wisely, as it turned out, since the stampede for bargains was terrifying).

In the nature of things ministers wield power available to few of their fellow citizens. Though (even after the 1996 salary increases) not paid especially well, they receive privileged treatment which, while on the whole required to enable them to carry out their necessary and generally useful jobs efficiently, can be morally debilitating if not seen, and seen through, for what it is – the perquisite of a temporary placeman subject to the whims of an electorate which can be severe and even capricious. Provided that you accept all that goes with your appointment as being the terms and conditions of an unusually interesting job which you are exceptionally lucky to have but which may be taken away from you at any time, no great damage will be done. But if you think that you really have a right to these privileged conditions, and forget what you are there to do and the people you are there to help, then ministerialitis will lay you low and you will be good for nothing, least of all the ministerial office which has so morbidly infected you.

Departmentalitis is a very different kind of disease, which can be contracted separately from ministerialitis but is quite often symbiotic with it. It stems from a preoccupation with the department to which the minister is assigned, to the exclusion of all other considerations including the fortunes of the government as a whole. If you are a minister afflicted with departmentalitis you will regard Parliament as existing only to further the interests of your department. You will show no interest in debates or question periods not relating to your own department's activities; even when your department's Question Time immediately precedes Prime Minister's Questions on Tuesdays and Thursdays, you will scoot off from the front bench as soon as your own last question has been reached, oblivious of the possibility that the Prime Minister might be likely to say something interesting.

If you contract departmentalitis you will ruthlessly pursue your own department's interests even if another department has a better case: quite simply, your department must win. You will often not even be interested in, let alone care, whether your department's activities impinge adversely on those of a colleague. When John Cunningham, as Under-Secretary of State for Energy, conducted a survey of the fuel efficiency of British cars and took care in advance that there should be no adverse effect on the Department of Industry's sponsorship of the car industry, he was showing himself dazzlingly departmentalitis-free.

If you contract departmentalitis you will go along to a Cabinet Committee determined to win, regardless of the merits of your colleagues' case. You will carry with you a brief which tells you the department's view, or explains the department's interest if this is not manifest. If you contract departmentalitis you will forget that you are part of a government, that the fortunes of the government are more important than the fortunes of your own department, that the fortunes of the government may well require that your own department's interests be subordinated to those of another. You are working so hard (only hard-working ministers suffer from departmentalitis), you are so immersed in your work, that you forget why you are there in the first place – to benefit the country and, incidentally, your own party, by assisting your government to be successful.

That you should be prone to this ailment is not surprising. After all, the department is where you spend most of your time. Your office is there, your staff is there, your officials are there. Your day is full of meetings in which officials who are quite certainly interested only in the activities of their own department will unthinkingly communicate to you their own monomania. One of my most sane and sensible fellow ministers once failed to turn up for a meeting arranged to be held in my department because his officials were so apprehensive of the sinister aura emanating from it that they feared that their minister would be dialectically seduced. After waiting with some impatience for my colleague and his advisers to arrive, I asked the reason for the delay. I was told that the other department had notified mine that the meeting would not be taking place unless it could be held on 'neutral ground'; it might almost have been the peace negotiations at Panmunjom. I sent a message reminding my colleague, in case it had slipped his mind, that we were members of the same government with identical interests and that, unless I heard from him swiftly, I would be moving off in the direction of his department accompanied by my own advisers (who regarded the entire absurd situation as perfectly reasonable). My colleague arrived fairly speedily and since he was not only sane and sensible but very clever too, we solved the problem in a matter of minutes. His officials, however, held the entire episode against me, and found ways of punishing me for years afterwards.

Some of the effects of departmentalitis can be extremely disquieting. Ministers can be persuaded by factitious arguments from their officials to advocate the purchase of foreign machinery or equipment – for 'departmental' reasons – when such purchases are damaging to British industrial interests. Ministers can be induced to refuse some trifling assistance to a project simply because their own departmental budget might be affected; an impasse on which department should pay for the construction of certain specialist ships important to the British shipbuilding industry was solved only when the relevant ministers met without their officials, threw away their departmental briefs, and decided to do what they all agreed was best for the country.

When, at the Department of Industry, I made a few anodyne remarks in the House of Commons about the need to impose fewer forms on industry to fill in, I aroused immense perturbation among the officials principally responsible for compiling these forms, who regarded my statements as contrary to departmental interests. The assault was so fierce, and delivered with such righteous conviction, that after a time I began to feel that I had indeed behaved disgracefully in being insufficiently loyal to the form-compilers and having the nerve to speak in Parliament without previously obtaining their agreement to my form of words. This incipient very severe attack of departmentalitis was fortunately dispelled by a sudden edict from the Prime Minister instructing that measures should be taken to cut down the number of burdensome forms.

Of course, it is necessary for you to pursue the interests of your department; that is why you are there. And little can arouse greater pleasure in a department than the return from a Cabinet Committee of a minister who has gained a majority for his departmental view. But you should always remember that you are a member of the government first, and a departmental representative second. That way, departmentalitis can be warded off.

If you are free of both ministerialitis and departmentalitis you cannot be certain that you will, for that reason alone, be effective or successful. As we shall see, there are many other hazards that you will encounter. But if you are afflicted by either of these political diseases, your effectiveness will be severely reduced. If you succumb to both, all the many talents that you may possess will make things worse, not better, since they will be employed for negative ends, not to increase the chances of success of the government to which you have been appointed by a Prime Minister whose office in Downing Street is not a department at all.

3

How to Begin

―――――

When you enter your new department you will be nervous; under-standably so, since you will be approaching a new experience and assuming a heavy responsibility. Be comforted by the knowledge that those who await you will be at least as nervous as you are.

Waiting at the threshold (together with the bacilli of ministerial-itis and departmentalitis) will be your Private Secretary. Every minister, of whatever rank, has a Private Office, adjoining his own office and manned by his own personal staff: for a junior minister, three or four, for a Cabinet minister many more. Of course they are not really his own choices. They are career civil servants assigned to Private Office work as part of their career structure, generally for two years or so. When his Principal Private Secretary (*the* Private Secretary) moves on in the normal course of events the minister (if he insists) will be able to choose the new one; the other members of the Private Office staff being selected in their turn by the Private Secretary. But the Private Secretary – male or female, the Civil Service happily not being sexist – who greets the minister on his first day in office will have been appointed by the outgoing minister, a member of the new minister's own party if he has been appointed as the result of a reshuffle, a member of the opposing party if the change comes because of a general election victory. Whoever appointed him, he is in charge of your personal domain, ready to anticipate and pander to your every whim and also to keep a sharp eye on you in case you show signs of getting out of line; if Big Brother is not watching you, Permanent Secretary certainly is. Your Private Secretary, or one of his assistants, will accompany you to all your engagements except Cabinet Committees, take a note of all your meetings, listen in to all your telephone conversations, travel with you at home and abroad. He will get to know you better than anyone except your close relatives.

The Private Secretary will first of all tell you his name which, in your confusion and nervousness, you will immediately forget. But it is important that you remember at least his Christian name, since that is what you will call him. It is a curious tradition of Private Office work that the Private Secretary operates solely on the basis of his Christian name. He signs notes to his minister (innumerable, day upon day) only with his Christian name. When he answers the telephone he answers with his Christian name. Having misheard it in the confusion of arrival, I did not find out my new Private Secretary's surname for quite some time; his Christian name, though (Jack, appropriate to the admirable ruffian from Barnsley he turned out to be) was easily remembered.

Your Private Secretary, however, will not presume to call you by your Christian name in return. To him you are always 'Minister' or 'Mr X'. Indeed, the use of names between ministers and the civil service is one of the most subtle and, in its way, pleasing manifestations of the British class system. Everyone, to begin with, will start by calling you 'Minister'. Gradually, as they get to know you, there will be a relaxation. Among senior civil servants the hierarchy rises (in ascending order): Assistant Secretary, Under-Secretary, Deputy Secretary, Permanent Secretary (the last of these, in the Department of Industry at any rate, being referred to austerely, impressively, and for no reason that I could ever understand, as 'the Secretary'). Up to and including Under-Secretary they will always call you 'Minister', however closely you work together and however well you get on. The officials (collective name for civil servants) at the Department of Industry included an Assistant Secretary whom I knew well, since he had been a fellow officer with me at Oxford University Labour Club twenty-five years before; even so, he never called me anything but 'Minister'. On the other hand I always called him 'David', addressing other civil servants of his rank also by their Christian names.

Deputy Secretaries and Permanent Secretaries will, though, exchange Christian names with you. You may regard these strange tribal customs as inherently absurd, and you may well be right. But try to interfere with them, and you will be in danger of blowing away with your thoughtless wind of change a house of cards whose delicate structure provides an atmosphere of certainty and continuity to those who built it. In any case, the whole ritual is purely temporary. Once he has moved away from service in your office, and provided he is not working for you in some other capacity, the most junior ex-Private Secretary will airily call you by your Christian name if he runs into you. And when you leave office, no holds are barred – that is, if he bothers to acknowledge you at all. In any case, this of course is only what officials call you to your face. Behind your back is a whole world of intrigue which puts *Upstairs, Downstairs* in the shade.

Your driver is in an entirely different category. He is not an employee of the department where you are a minister but of the Government Car Service (GCS), for which the Office of Public Service is now responsible. That responsibility previously rested with the Department of the Environment (DoE) and, when I was at the DoE, supreme authority over the GCS rested with me, a position of greater power than anyone except the Prime Minister himself enjoys. The allocation of cars to ministers arouses violent emotions (more among the drivers than the ministers). When I entered the government, the fleet of ministerial cars consisted of Rovers and Wolseleys, and everyone wanted a Rover. Since there was a shortage of these, I decided arbitrarily that only Cabinet ministers could have Rovers, a clear and readily comprehensible rule. This decision was accepted as fair, provided it was universally adhered to. But one day I was summoned by Fred Mulley, at that time a non-Cabinet minister (I went to his office, since he was senior to me), who without beating about the bush demanded that he be allocated a Rover. I carefully explained the rule to him, but he was mistrustful. 'How is it that David Owen' – another minister then not in the Cabinet – 'is getting one, then?' he demanded. All became clear to me. Owen had indeed applied for a Rover, on the ingenious and heart-rending ground that Wolseleys made him car sick and rendered him unfit for his ministerial duties. I had hard-heartedly refused, brusquely suggesting that what he needed was not a new car but medical treatment. This explanation was accepted by Fred, a good-natured man who nevertheless was not ready to be put upon.

Pleas for special vehicular favours came thick and fast. Reginald Prentice was, for some reason, often first in the field, for example in his request (granted) for the supply of a radio telephone, at that time an advanced and privileged means of communication. I do not know why he wanted one. I had to have one during the period in which I was seconded to the Cabinet Office for the strike emergency of early 1979, and found it a great nuisance. My greatest test came, however, when 10 Downing Street demanded that the Prime Minister's new Rover be re-upholstered in Harris tweed. Knowing Harold Wilson's unassuming personal tastes, I was somewhat surprised by this sybaritic manifestation, particularly when I had the re-upholstering costed and found it to be very expensive indeed. I vetoed it, and waited for the explosion. None came. Harold Wilson, as I had suspected, knew nothing whatever about it. Harris tweed upholstery for Prime Ministerial cars turned out, on investigation, to have been a tradition instituted by Harold Macmillan, no doubt as a memento of his simple crofting antecedents, and the request for it to be continued had come from the Downing Street machine operating on autopilot.

A minister will, however, if he is sensible, do a great deal to please his driver, since he is heavily dependent upon him. Some ministers are highly offensive to their drivers and consequently find it very difficult to get anyone to drive them; some run through a succession of increasingly reluctant and sullen recipients of the GCS black spot. Others, like Richard Crossman, Tony Benn and Harold Wilson, build up strong personal relationships with their drivers. A driver is always known to the minister by his Christian name, and I was exceptionally fortunate with the two I had, the first a young woman who retired to get married, the second accompanying me from DoE to the Department of Industry and remaining with me until I was dismissed by the electorate.

If this driver had a flaw, it was the virtuous one of being liable to disappear at a moment's notice to attend meetings of the Transport and General Workers' Union, which is very strong in the Government Car Service, and in which he personally was a great power. He always took pains to find me a substitute, but sometimes these did not live up to his own high standards. One, for example, could not be found anywhere when I needed to go out to a ministerial lunch appointment, and a substitute substitute had to be provided; upon investigation it turned out that the original substitute had, logically enough from his point of view it must be admitted, gone off to his own lunch. Sometimes my driver's absences grew so inconveniently frequent that I contemplated asking him to choose between me and the Transport and General Workers' Union. I refrained for two reasons: first, because in those days it would have been unseemly for a socialist to put such a choice to anyone; second, because he would unhesitatingly have chosen the Transport and General Workers' Union.

It is of course essential that your driver and Private Office get on well, since they have to work closely together. It is the Private Office that prepares your red box, but your driver who will bring it to your home. Your Private Office will give your driver your daily diary, and he will then be expected to deliver you to the places listed on it at the times specified. All these arcana will, of course, be ahead of you as you step across the threshold of your new Department to be greeted by Jack, Joan, John, Shirley, or whoever it may be.

You will be taken up first to see the Permanent Secretary. All future meetings with him will be held in your own office, to which he will be on call and where he will arrive just a little late, to show that he is not just anybody. But the first meeting, at any rate for a junior minister, is in the Permanent Secretary's office which, like that of a minister, has its outer office manned by a Private Office staff. The Department of the Environment, being a mammoth institution, had inexhaustible supplies of Permanent Secretaries, but I saw the daddy of them all, a man whom Richard Crossman lauded in his diaries as possessed of a great intellect. I never got a real chance to find out, since I only met him once more, at the party held the following year to speed me on my way to exile at the Department of Industry. On this occasion he made a little speech, forecasting that one day I would return to the Department of the Environment as Secretary of State, thus confirming, as far as I was concerned, everything that Crossman had said about his intellect but also confirming that, regrettably, he lacked accurate powers of prophecy.

At this introductory meeting, however, the Permanent Secretary gave me a brief explanation of the way the department operated, wished me good fortune, and passed speedily on to no doubt more important matters, putting me in the charge of my Private Secretary (whom he named wrongly, himself not really needing to know the right name). We then proceeded to my own office where the rest of my personal staff were waiting to meet me, no doubt – in common with the Private Secretary himself and all the officials who would have to work with me – in fear and trembling. Because the question in the minds of all civil servants who suddenly find themselves encumbered with a new minister is, quite starkly: 'What have we got here?' The new minister may turn out to be rude, lazy, irascible, dirty, a drunkard or – worst of all – stupid. And they are stuck with him, particularly the Private Office, who have to live with him all the time. To begin with, they operate on the safest principle, namely that he is an imbecile.

It is the safest principle because, whatever the minister's incompetences, the show must go on. Letters must be signed, meetings must be attended, delegations must be seen, parliamentary questions must be dealt with, debates answered, bills steered through to the statute book. The civil service has built-in protective mechanisms for every eventuality and, unless you show pretty quickly that you do not need them or do not want them, they will in the most benevolent way proceed to turn you into a pod straight out of *Invasion of the Body Snatchers*.

First there is the choice of the Private Secretary himself. A few weeks after my arrival at the Department of the Environment I was told that the Establishments Officer wanted to see me. He arrived, and announced with the greatest confidentiality and good will that he had a new Private Secretary for me. I responded that I had a Private Secretary already and that, while of course he would have to move on after a while, I was not ready for a change while I was still finding my feet. This was an unexpected act of defiance. It turned out that the Establishments Office had a chap just come back from a tour of duty in Hong Kong, and they needed to find somewhere to put him. My office was regarded as a useful receptacle, and the only snag was me. Despite the Establishments Officer's determined pressure I continued to persist in being a snag and, after several further attempts, he gave up. His office retaliated, when the time did come for me to choose my Private Secretary's successor, by sending along a series of highly unsuitable candidates. I rejected them all, and in the end was offered someone of top quality whom I accepted with alacrity. Moral: never let anyone but yourself choose your Private Secretary. If you get the wrong one life can be hell for you and for him.

Next there is the question of the diary. Every evening you are given a piece of card to put in your pocket, telling you what you will be doing all the next day. A fortnightly advance diary is deposited in your box each weekend. He who controls the minister's diary controls his life. So it had better be you. There is, of course, a Diary Secretary, one of the Private Office staff. A good rule right from the start is to inform the Diary Secretary that nothing whatever can go into your diary without your own express permission. This may sound elementary but it is vital. Into the office of every minister, however junior, there rolls a constant stream of invitations. Even if they disagree with your government's policies, every trade association likes to have a ministerial representative to grace its lunch or dinner. So you will be constantly invited to be guest of honour at the annual lunch of the Concrete Mixers' Benevolent Association or dinner of the Guild of Roof Tiling Employers.

These events are even more boring than they sound. Reject them all. Otherwise, one mealtime you will find yourself to your dismay sitting in a huge dining room at the Hilton or the Dorchester – these associations do themselves well – desperately trying to make conversation over the prawn cocktail (in my days at Downing Street Mary Wilson and I used to have bets at official functions as to whether the first course would be prawn cocktail covered with an impenetrably thick sauce or a diced section of honeydew melon surmounted by a slice of orange on a plastic flag) with someone you have never met before and devoutly hope you will never meet again. Some of these hosts could be very strange. One, for a whole lunch time, insisted on addressing the Assistant Private Secretary who accompanied me, a very sensitive young man with impressive academic qualifications, as 'Christopher Robin'. All of them, when the time came for post-prandial speeches, would launch into vehement if occasionally ungrammatical denunciations of the policies of the government represented at their celebration by their guest of honour. A very little experience of this led me to refuse almost all such invitations, and my delightful Diary Secretary (a lovely girl called Angela, who has since married and still sends me Christmas cards from Bolton) soon learned to turn them down without even consulting me.

It is not only lunches and dinners, however; you must keep control of every engagement that you make. Because, after all, your Diary Secretary has a job to do, and that job is arranging engagements. He or she will therefore, unless halted, proceed to make engagements until, as one of my colleagues pathetically put it, you will not be able to get a razor blade between them. This makes for fatigue. It also leaves very little time for all the other things you have to do. These include dealing with letters. Much of this correspondence is with ministerial colleagues, and this will be discussed in a later chapter. A good deal more is with civil servants in your own department, and this too will be examined presently. But there will be letters pouring in from Members of Parliament, from trade unions, trade associations, interest groups, and, plain and simple, members of the general public. It is physically impossible for the minister to answer all of these himself, so it is necessary to work out a system. Every minister will have his own.

A useful categorization is for routine letters, including those from cranks, to be answered by the relevant policy division; and for letters of more substance, such as those from parliamentary candidates of an opposing party, to be answered by the Private Secretary. The Department of the Environment, when I first got there, had a practice that titled persons, whatever their qualifications, got a reply from the minister; but I put a stop to that. I myself – though other ministers may have handled it differently – signed letters to all Members of Parliament, including peers, all trade unions and associations, and all prospective Labour candidates and Labour Party branches, as well as of course to Labour Party headquarters itself. I say 'signed' because, of course, there was not time for me to dictate them all. All incoming letters would be submitted to me in a folder, and I would go through them marking those for which special replies were necessary. A handful I would take out to dictate replies myself. The rest would go down to the appropriate policy division for a draft to be prepared.

When I arrived at DoE, replies used to come to me on ministerial headed notepaper ready for signature and transmission. There was thus tremendous pressure on the minister to sign the letter and let it go; to alter it was to interfere with a beautifully prepared top copy, not to mention the extra expense of getting it done again. But, since civil servants had got used to preparing replies acceptable to a Conservative minister, many of the letters were unacceptable and had to be sent back all the same. So we evolved the practice of my being sent rough drafts, with which I could tamper without having a bad conscience about it.

25

Your letters will be presented to you for signature either on your desk or in your red box. Other items will come before you in the same way. Even if you are very junior you will have small but quite important decisions to make. And some of the decisions will be very important indeed. In the Housing Division of the Department of the Environment the Under-Secretary of State had delegated to him by the Secretary of State authority to make decisions on all contested compulsory purchase orders, excepting very major ones and excluding those relating to his own constituency. Generally the view, rightly, was that the Secretary of State should uphold the inspector's report. Otherwise, why have an inspector's report? But on the other hand, in that case why have a ministerial decision? I – like no doubt my predecessors and successors – went into these matters in meticulous detail, aware that the quality of life of whole neighbourhoods was at stake. From my own constituency work I knew that demolition of small shops and businesses can take away all sense of identity from an area, and I therefore was always particularly painstaking with such propositions. I remember being especially concerned with the fate of a Yorkshire fish and chip shop, which in the end I rescued from destruction.

Doing your box is something that you have to do, because no one else can do it for you. No one's signature but yours is acceptable (or sometimes legal) on letters or documents or decisions. Your Private Secretary will work hard clearing away all the irrelevant detail, but in the end you must do the box. If you leave it, it will simply pile up with others piling up on top of that. If you send it back unmarked every document you fail to sign or at least tick will relentlessly turn up again.

So there are two rules which are essential right at the beginning of your stint of duty as a minister. First, be your own master. You will make mistakes, some of them serious. But it is better to make your own mistakes than someone else's. Second, do your work and do it systematically. And remember, only if you are in control of your own office and your own timetable will you be ready for the next challenge: the Whitehall machine.

4

How to Operate the System

It lurks there in your own department. Its tentacles link your department with all the other departments, via the government telecommunications network. The eyes watching it all are the eyes of 10 Downing Street; but the controlling brain is the Cabinet Office. It is the system, and either you will learn how to use it, or it will use you.

I do not know where they meet, but all civil servants seem to know each other. On three occasions the Prime Minister put me in charge of inter-departmental groups of officials which met frequently to conduct surveys into selected areas of policy. For two months I was seconded to the Cabinet Office, where I had regular meetings with officials of many Departments. On each occasion, at the first meeting, I was amazed to find that, for example, officials from the Welsh Office were closely acquainted with those of the Department of Energy, that those from the Ministry of Defence (a very special breed) knew those from the Department of Employment equally well. This of course put me at an immediate disadvantage, as being the odd man out always does.

The system has its own stately rituals. One of the most formalized relates to communications between officials and Ministers. Officials will put an issue to ministers in a document known as a 'submission'. Some officials are exceptionally prolific with submissions. The most prolific I ever knew – I suspect the most prolific there ever has been or possibly ever will be – was a superb Deputy Secretary at the Department of Industry – brilliant, inventive, humorous, loyal – called Ron Dearing. When my Private Secretary used to tell me that a submission was on its way up from Mr Dearing – for Private Secretaries know in advance everything that is going to happen – my reply would simply be, 'of course'. I once even contemplated writing a novel in the style of E.M. Forster called *A Submission from Mr Dearing*. It was eventually decided that Ron Dearing's formidable if idiosyncratic skills could be put to more fruitful use and he was appointed head of the nation's postal services, so reaching his apotheosis in supervising the safe and speedy transmission and delivery of other people's submissions and kindred written communications; but that was far from the end of his hyperactive role in the nation's life. When Camelot launched the National Lottery it was Dearing who, as its chairman, awarded to the organisation the priceless prize of obvious, almost blatant, integrity. Dearing also became the Conservative government's educational Pooh-bah, turned to as the last, reliable resort when schools or universities had reached the end of their own tether.

Official submissions will have three distinguishing features. The first will be the copy list situated neatly down the right-hand side of the page. The more important the submission, the shorter the list of people to whom it will be copied. Some submissions have copy lists so long that they stretch right down the page; they inevitably turn out to be boring. A submission – preferably a top copy on blue paper, rather than a turgid photocopy – simply copied to 'Secretary of State' and 'Secretary' can be guaranteed to have some meat in it. The next feature of importance is the security classification. This can range, in ascending order of importance, from Restricted, through Confidential (or Commercially Confidential, if business secrets are involved) to Secret. I believe there is a Top Secret as well, but one of those never came my way. According to my own private system of classification Restricted was the kind of thing no newspaper would bother to publish, Confidential was interesting enough to warrant a couple of paragraphs in the *Daily Mail*, while Secret would rate an insight story in *The Sunday Times* or one of those *Observer* probes.

The third distinguishing feature of a submission is the form of address it employs (assuming, that is, that it is addressed direct to your office rather than addressed to another office and simply copied to yours). The superscription will either be, say, Minister of State (or Mr X) or PS/Minister of State. PS stands for Private Secretary. A submission addressed thus indicates that it comes from an official too lowly to presume to address the minister direct in correspondence. I never did get this matter absolutely settled in my own mind, but came to the conclusion that officials who sent PS submissions were those who would not call you by your Christian name to your face, namely those proceeding from Under-Secretaries downwards.

There are, however, added complications which, if you are not careful, can send your mind reeling. You may decide to send a minute (never a submission, which is for officials only) to the Secretary of State of your own department. He will certainly read it. It is highly improbable, however, that he will reply direct. Instead the likelihood is that your Private Secretary will receive a minute from his Private Secretary beginning, 'The Secretary of State has seen your minister's minute, and . . .' In correspondence with ministers in other departments you will generally stick to your own class, ministers of state writing to other ministers of state and so forth, though in certain circumstances a junior minister may write to a Secretary of State and even get a reply from him. It is also open to you, if you think it worth stirring him up, to send a minute direct to the Prime Minister. The response will almost certainly be through his Private Secretary. If the Prime Minister himself sends you a Personal Minute, you really have made the big time (or, on the other hand, committed a massive error from which you may never recover).

Submissions are written in a language all their own. There are certain words without which a submission cannot achieve its full, ripe flavour – words without which, I suspect, a submission is not really valid. These are words which no human being will use in everyday life, and which never occur in literature read for pleasure: words like 'thus', 'hence' and 'hitherto'. One of the most imaginative officials who ever worked for me, a man who, for example, loved musicals and was a joy to converse with, was the biggest 'hencer' I have ever come across. Dr Jekyll in everyday life, he was transformed in the department into a Mr Hyde who with a malevolent leer would torture the English language into submission. There are other forms of jargon which, in my time in government, I did my best to expunge. These included requests for briefing to be supplied 'by close of play' – as if government were some kind of cricket match – and the use of the word 'host' as a verb, as in 'hosting' a reception. No doubt after my departure they sprang up again like caries-ridden dragons' teeth.

Submissions can come in all shapes and sizes. Submissions about

Concorde were so complicated – containing, as they generally did, preposterous but recondite claims from the French – that they were often accompanied by brief covering explanatory submissions, relieving you of the need to read the principal document: though it was as well for you to do so, since frightening details would thus (you see, I'm at it myself) come to your attention. Most submissions, however, consist of three or four pages, containing a concise summary of a problem with possible courses of action completing the document. Some officials will just suggest one course of action, for you to take or leave. Others, more cunning, will attempt to confuse you with a choice, while carefully steering you in the direction they want you to go. The key, of course, is not necessarily to accept any of the courses of action they recommend, but to come up with some others yourself. The really inventive minister will even reject the very problem posed to him, and map out another and more politically attractive scenario.

You should bear in mind that officials are likely to send you submissions about subjects that interest them rather than those that interest you. Indeed, though you may suddenly become concerned about some matter and ask for a submission about it, if the officials involved think you are just making a nuisance of yourself they will forget all about it, and only take action when you nag or threaten them into doing so. At the Department of Industry on one occasion two issues arose, on one of which officials were agog for action while I was not very interested at all, while on the other I wanted something done against complete indifference by officials. I won by letting it be known (through the invaluable Private Secretary) that I would take no action on their item unless they jumped to it on mine.

You can react to a submission in various ways. One is to write on it: 'I agree with Mr Dearing' (or whoever it might be, but it is usually Mr Dearing) 'and accept his advice.' Another is to write: 'This is all nonsense, and we should do so-and-so.' A third, if you cannot make up your mind straight away, is to write: 'We must have a meeting.' Of course, if you reject the official advice you may be asked by the spurned official to have a meeting anyhow, so that he can persuade you face to face of what his written submission failed to convince you. It is best to get this meeting over quickly, because while acceptance of official advice will be followed by instantaneous action, rejection will lead to a rearguard action so skilled as to leave you breathless with admiration (and fury).

Meetings are occasions of quite a ceremonial nature. Officials will gather in your outer office (often making mysterious telephone calls there), carrying bulky and rather untidy-looking files. Even if the issue is thought by you to be only between you and the author of the submission, he will very likely bring several of his colleagues along, either to supply supporting evidence or (I sometimes suspected) simply to intimidate you. Some of these officials you may never have seen before; some of them, possibly, do not even have names. But, in an order or hierarchy they will have decided by instinct – like a flight of starlings – they will gather round your table and begin. With exceptions, of course, they are generally people of high quality. They have a capacity for total recall that always left me gasping and which seems to be taught in the civil service at an early age, since all Private Secretaries have it, as proved by the notes of meetings that they make. The Private Secretary himself attends the meeting though pretending not to be really there, since active participation might force him to take sides (if pressed, he will side with his minister), and instead sits in a corner taking his note, occasionally leaving the room to carry out the act of telephoning which is compulsive for all Private Secretaries. Occasionally, too, an Assistant Private Secretary will enter the room to give the Private Secretary a little note or whisper into his ear; he never tells you what this is about.

The arguments are hammered out, and in the end you get a decision. But that may not be the end of the story. Other departments may have an interest, and the whole weary process has to be gone through again. Sometimes, of course, another department turns out to have an interest because your own officials want it that way. If they themselves cannot persuade their minister, they bring up reinforcements.

One morning you will say to your Private Secretary, 'Has that decision about (say) the rescue of the paper-mill gone through?' to be told: 'The Treasury is worried about it.' Interpreted, this is liable to mean that the official whose advice you have rejected has got in touch with his counterpart at the Treasury and said something to him along the lines of: 'That idiot Kaufman insists on paying out money to rescue a decrepit paper-mill. Can you help us to stop him?' The next development will follow swiftly. 'Mr X has asked to see you,' your Private Secretary will one day announce, referring to the relevant official. 'Yes, of course, when would he like to come?' you reply in that accommodating fashion you have culti-vated, to be trumped by the response: 'He's waiting outside now.' The official will then enter, and mournfully report that in spite of his valiant efforts the Treasury have vetoed your paper-mill project.

He is now hoping that you will do one of two things: either accept defeat with good grace or, if that is too much to expect, ask him to draft you a letter of protest to send to the Chief Secretary to the Treasury, who is in charge of all public expenditure. If you are wise you will do neither of these things. Because if you decide to write to the Chief Secretary, all that will happen is that your letter will go straight to the Treasury official who is conniving with your own official to do you down. He will then draft a rather nasty refusal which will in due course be submitted to the Chief Secretary, who will almost certainly sign it, since he has several dozen such matters clamouring for his attention at any one time.

Instead, what you will do if you are wise is to say offhandedly that you will think about it and then, in the Division Lobby at the House of Commons that night, get hold of the Chief Secretary, tell him the problem and persuade him to agree to your course of action. You will then wander into your office the next morning and, while exchanging the time of day with your Private Secretary, casually announce that you saw the Chief Secretary last night and got him to agree to your paper-mill project. Game, set and match to you, and your officials will have to think of a new one next time. The one thing they can never cope with is action by you on the political network, to which they do not have access and which, with all their undoubted skill and sometimes brilliance, they cannot understand.

Do not believe, however, that you should spend your time in government in conflict with officials and chalking up victories against them. That course of action may convince you of your own machismo, but it will not get you a very long way with Whitehall. Of course, if you cannot carry the system with you, you must find ways of circumventing it or even defeating it. But you cannot continue like this indefinitely. If you attempt to do so the system will very gently but very firmly circumvent you and extrude you from its workings, as it once did for a time with an entire government department, the Department of Industry, during the period when Tony Benn was Secretary of State. It is essential most of the time to carry the system with you, so that it will accept your decisions even when it does not agree with them.

And that means, to begin with, that you must treat your civil servants with courtesy and respect. They have great experience and skill which they can place at your disposal. They may not agree with you politically (though very many will) but they really do have a sense of loyalty to their ministers. Some ministers – Richard Crossman was one – pride themselves on having rows with their officials. But it is very easy and rather unpleasant to have rows with people who in the nature of things cannot answer you back. Any minister can occasionally lose his temper, and no one will mind. But systematic rudeness is remembered and resented. One of the most powerful networks in Whitehall is the Private Office grapevine – another, even more active though not always so reliable, being that of the ministerial drivers – and that rang for weeks with the story of the junior minister who turned up extremely early at his department one day to find that none of his Private Office had yet arrived. When they did, he called them all in and instructed each of them to write him a personal letter explaining why they had not been there in time to serve him. That minister found it very difficult indeed to get proper co-operation in his activities.

On the other hand, if they really want to help, officials can find ways not only round substantive difficulties but also round procedural problems. When I was given responsibility for the steel industry I came, after careful thought, to the conclusion that I would oppose any proposed closure of the Shotton steelworks in North Wales. I held a series of meetings with officials, who put at my disposal all the information I needed, and I arrived at the view that while the case for closure at Shotton was considerable, it was far from conclusively proven. I decided to minute the Secretary of State accordingly. Almost all my officials disagreed with me, and I thought it right that the Secretary of State should know of their disagreement. I therefore invited the responsible Deputy Secretary to send him a minute setting out his own contrary views. The Secretary of State considered the matter and endorsed my recommended course of action. At a further meeting with very senior officials he confirmed this, and then told the officials that, while he knew they disagreed, he looked for their help in implementing the ministerial decision. They responded with complete and loyal co-operation, and the decision was consequently endorsed by the necessary government machinery.

If they had decided to work against it, they could have stirred up a hornets' nest. Other ministers, for their own valid reasons, might have had their reservations in any case. Prodded by their own top officials, who would have been prodded in their turn by ours, they might have turned this issue into a major Cabinet controversy, the outcome of which could have been in doubt and might have gone against us.

Pitfalls awaited me when I was put in charge of inter-depart-mental committees of officials, since any one of those officials could have obstructed me by telling his own minister that I was disre-garding their department's interests. I therefore took great trouble to ensure that every department felt it was being treated fairly. The dangers were even greater when James Callaghan sent me early in 1979 to work under the Home Secretary in the Cabinet Office during the rash of strikes in road haulage and the public services. Not only were some of the most basic departmental interests at stake here – a fit breeding ground for an epidemic of ministerialitis – but this was a rare occasion of a minister being brought in to supervise a responsibility of the august Cabinet Office itself. I realized that I must tread carefully if a whole power structure was not to feel itself threatened.

If the Whitehall machine as a whole is a Daimler, stately and effective, the Cabinet Office is a Ferrari, built for speed and action. High-flyers from other departments are seconded from time to time, and the general quality of the personnel, though it varies, can be dazzling. It services the Prime Minister and knows his wishes. It is in constant contact with all government departments and is aware of everything that is going on there. Almost at the drop of a hat, it can produce documents, aircraft, communications networks, plans. Whereas government departments are situated in imposing buildings (some of them of devastating hideousness) the Cabinet Office inhabits rather shabby rooms reached through a doorway in Whitehall which you scarcely notice when you pass it. If the

Cabinet Office is against you, you have little hope. If it is on your side, you have a possibly conclusive advantage.

Many who have been in government have a hearty dislike of the Whitehall machine. Many who have not been in government regard Whitehall as a sinister conspiracy against elected government. Socialists believe it is anti-socialist. Radical Tories fear its suspected tendency towards consensus. What Whitehall does believe in, for better or for worse, is continuity. If convinced of the need for action on practical grounds, it will assist Labour governments to advance socialism – it was desperate, for example, to get shipbuilding nationalized – and will equally impartially assist Conservative governments to demolish what the socialists have created. Often the same officials will do both. The officials at the Department of the Environment who participated in constructing the Housing Finance Act in 1972 were on hand in 1975 to aid in its effective repeal. The officials at the Department of Industry who assisted Labour ministers in 1975 to launch the National Enterprise Board were there in 1979 to help castrate it. This can be admired as impartiality or denounced as cynicism. More likely it is a mixture of both.

The question that civil servants ask themselves when required to advise in implementing polemical proposals is not, 'Do I agree with it?' but, 'Can it be made to work?' If they think it can, they will help to make it work. If they think it cannot, they will do their best to stop it. This is not a very heroic posture, and it can be very irritating, even maddening. Politicians who want to excite the country with imaginative proposals find them watered down in the interests of practicality. And when you become involved with the Whitehall machine, you will find that to satisfy it you have to answer as many questions as you ask. It is suspicious of innovations. It never really took to Edward Heath's Central Policy Review Staff, though this was in fact a valuable creation designed to look at problems from an involved but non-departmental point of view.

Be sure of this: when you become a minister, the system will be there waiting for you and watching you. Antagonize it, and you can do little. Win its co-operation, and you can do quite a lot. But nobody has yet worked out a method of harnessing it to achieve the fulfilment of a complete and cohesive political programme. If you can find a way of doing that, you will not only learn how to be a minister, you will find yourself catapulted into 10 Downing Street.

5
How to Make Policy

———

You are in government because you are in Parliament. You have been elected to Parliament in an election which your party has won. Your party has won the election on the basis of a manifesto submitted to the electorate, though very few of them will have read it. The manifesto itself is the distillation of policies worked out by your party during the years of Opposition. You want to carry it out.

Be sure of one thing. When you enter your department after your election victory, your officials will know at least as much about your policies as you do. They will have studied all your party's policy pronouncements, read all its pamphlets. More than that, they will have spent the months leading up to the election preparing actively for your arrival, just in case you win. Indeed, several of them will have been relieved of their routine tasks in order to make such preparations in detail. That is why Whitehall was ready for Labour in 1974 and equally ready for the Conservatives in 1979. When your Private Secretary has sat you down at your desk with a cup of departmental tea or coffee, he will carry in a mass of situation papers that have been prepared ready for this very moment.

When you attend your initial meetings with departmental officials they will all enter bearing copies of your manifesto and related documents. In 1964 Tony Benn, as Postmaster-General, distributed copies of the Labour Party's election manifesto throughout his department, following a precedent set by Hugh Dalton at the Foreign Office a third of a century before. Dalton may have needed to; Benn almost certainly did not. When in March 1974 I walked into the minister's queasily decorated room for my first meeting on housing policy I found myself surrounded by officials bearing like talismans not only the Labour Party election manifesto but also the policy booklet *Labour's Programme 1973*. They were particularly knowledgeable about municipalization, their zeal for which, I soon discovered, had little to do with Socialist principles but a great deal to do with the 40,000 privately built houses for which builders could not find customers in the then current mortgage famine. The problem was quickly solved, partly by inducing local authorities to buy the houses (municipalization) and partly by an ingenious plan to end the mortgage famine by lending the building societies money, worked out by Anthony Crosland and Harold Lever.

So it all sounds very easy. You know the policy. You have access to expert technical assistance. If you do not proceed to carry out the contents of the manifesto lock, stock and barrel, the party will know whom to blame. There are, unfortunately, snags. First, though your party may form the government, it may not have a working majority in Parliament. Much is made of Labour's eleven years in office between 1964 and 1979; but for seven of those years Labour never had an overall majority of more than five seats, and for most of that time had no majority at all. And of course throughout the period it was in a minority in the House of Lords.

These difficulties are not always sufficiently taken into account. On one occasion, when Labour was firmly in the minority in the Commons, an ardently socialist friend insisted to me that the government simply must win a crucial division to be held in Parliament the following night. I promised to guarantee victory, provided he could find a few Labour MPs down his street that our Chief Whip did not know about.

Secondly, it is not always feasible to translate a line in a manifesto into meaningful action, however hard you try. Take, for example, the commitment in Labour's 1974 manifesto to 'provide for a system of planning agreements between the government and key companies to ensure that the plans of those companies are in harmony with national needs and objectives and that government financial assistance is deployed where it will be most effectively used'. Nothing sounds simpler – until, that is, you try to carry it out.

I entered the Department of Industry in June 1975 full of zest to implement the whole of Labour's industrial strategy as soon as possible. Since I had spent a year and a quarter involved in housing legislation at the Department of the Environment I was a little rusty on the latest developments in industrial policy, and therefore asked my Private Secretary if someone could just write down on a piece of paper for me a definition of a planning agreement. I sat back and waited expectantly. Nothing happened. In the fifteen months during which Labour had held office with a commitment to introduce planning agreements, nobody seemed to have sat down and worked out what should actually go into a planning agreement, even though a Bill to empower their introduction was at that very moment before Parliament.

Others had their firm ideas, of course. Delegations of workers, deeply concerned to avoid impending redundancies at their factories, would ask for the urgent introduction of a planning agreement with their company in order to stave off these redundancies. Planning agreements had never, however, been contemplated as solutions for short-term emergencies. The whole point of them was that they should be not last-minute devices for warding off a crisis, but part of a long-term constructive relationship between government and individual companies. This might even involve anticipating redundancies as part of a long-term restructuring. Leading trade unionists saw this very well. They did not want to touch planning agreements with a barge-pole. In principle they were ardently in favour of introducing them. But the TUC, asked if unions at national level would like to be signatories to planning agreements, flinched slightly and hastened to decline the invitation with thanks.

There was also the question of how planning agreements, once we had found out what they were, should be introduced. Many Labour Members of Parliament felt that they should be imposed compulsorily; and after four years of trying to gain voluntary acceptance of them, I had much sympathy for this approach. The trouble was, they were called *agreements*. How do you compel somebody to agree and still claim they have agreed? In any case the Bill, introduced before I got to the department, clearly laid down that the agreements should be voluntary. This had been robustly confirmed by the then minister, Eric Heffer, in one of his characteristically forthright speeches, winding up the Second Reading debate of the enabling Bill itself. So, though the Bill was enacted and hundreds of hours were subsequently spent discussing potential planning agreements with various companies, by 1979 only two planning agreements had been signed.

One, with the National Coal Board, was the outcome of negotiations which Eric Varley as Secretary of State for Energy had instituted long before the enabling Bill ever came before Parliament. The other was imposed as part of the Labour government's ill-fated rescue of Chrysler UK, and was so ineffectual that it failed even to give advance warning of so basic an event as the take-over of Chrysler by Peugeot-Citroën. At the end of Labour's period of office the planning agreement system, though in my view still of potentially great importance for the increasingly urgent regeneration of British industry, was a dead letter; it was difficult to understand why Sir Keith Joseph bothered to repeal the provision in his 1980 Industry Act. Yet this was a policy commitment on whose attempted fulfilment much time and effort had been spent. There was a moral somewhere.

There was a moral of a different kind in the outcome of efforts to fulfil another election commitment: the abolition of the excrescence of lump labour, a form of moonlighting which enabled unscrupulous employers to circumvent the most elementary legislation protecting workers in the building industry. John Silkin, as Minister for Planning and Local Government, was given responsibility for fulfilling this pledge and, with his customary energy, set about preparation for the necessary enabling legislation. Towards the end of this process I, being at the time between Bills and at something of a loose end, was assigned to assist in carrying the legislation through Parliament. I sat in on the final discussions and was therefore present to participate in the discovery that a Bill was not after all needed and that the abuse could be effectively stamped out by administrative action in co-operation with the Treasury. All that agonizing, in the drafting of the Labour Government's first Queen's Speech, as to whether Her Majesty should be asked to frame her royal lips round the gross word 'lump' (she was, and did it with much poise), was for nothing.

At the beginning of a Parliament you will indeed feel thwarted if deprived of the opportunity of a Bill. By the end, having learned how fatiguing the process of legislation can be, you will be deeply relieved. You will learn the virtue and efficiency of administrative action, which can often be carried out without reference to Parliament at all, and can sometimes be achieved by statutory instruments which take up very little parliamentary debating time, if any. In 1979 the Conservative government began solely by administrative action the implementation of their policy to reduce the numbers entering Britain of people then unashamedly described as 'coloured immigrants'. They continued in 1980 by tabling statutory rules that did not require parliamentary endorsement, and pleaded shortage of parliamentary time for their failure to fulfil some of their most contentious pledges, relating to quotas and a register for immigrants.

No doubt they had been told by Home Office officials that it simply could not be done. Because you will learn that when your officials oppose something strongly but are unable to advance political reason for their opposition, they will smother you with protestations as to why the thing is simply not possible technically. Disregard these objections. If a thing is worth doing a way can always be found. Eric Heffer – a Labour minister who found the process of government so time-consuming that after a while he simply abandoned it for a less constricting role on the back benches, from which he would criticize his successor for still being unable to do what he himself had been unable to do – would rapidly lose patience with his officials. When he asked them to carry out some instruction of his which they averred was impracticable, he would simply growl, 'It's for you to find a way,' dismiss them from the room in a lordly manner, and return to attending to the constituency correspondence which eternally preoccupied him.

He may have carried this rather far, but in essence he was right. In the previous chapter I used the rescue of a paper-mill as a passing example of Whitehall guile. I did not do so lightly, for I was myself involved in the rescue of a small paper-mill in Lancashire. Officials at the Department of Industry simply did not want to rescue this mill. They felt that to save it did not fit in with the government's industrial strategy, a concept which they ardently supported whenever they felt it could be called in evidence to support their own predilections (another example being their attempt to stifle before birth the National Enterprise Board's admirable plans for the manufacture of standard silicon chips). I told them that I wanted it to be saved; so did my fellow Minister of State; so did the Secretary of State himself. I put the most ingenious, not to say Machiavellian, of all senior Department of Industry civil servants personally in charge of the attempted rescue; all to no avail.

One day I decided to circumvent him. I telephoned a ministerial colleague at the Treasury – since the Treasury naturally had a financial interest – and discussed the matter at length, taking care roundly to abuse the Machiavellian civil servant for his laziness and incompetence. I counted on the Treasury minister's Private Secretary listening in to the conversation and circulating its some-what juicy contents on the grapevine. It worked. My objurgations reached the relevant official, as they were meant to, and he, put on his mettle, subordinated his formidable capacity for obstruction to his even greater powers of cunning contrivance, and soon came up with an effective rescue plan.

You will find that civil servants are very versatile performers. One day they will tell you that something that must be done cannot be done; the next they will insist that something must be done even though you do not want it to be done. They can be very persistent. Labour came to office in March 1974 on a commitment to limit rent increases for private tenants. Moving with impressive speed Anthony Crosland immediately imposed a rent freeze as a prelimi-nary to the enactment of the detailed legislation. Disquiet soon spread among officials. The rent freeze was proving irksome to certain landlords who, for example, included heating charges in the rent they charged. There was something in what the officials said – you will discover that there always is – but the problem was how to accommodate the requirements of this minority of landlords without undermining the effectiveness of the rent freeze in totality. Attempts were made to find a way but none succeeded, and Anthony Crosland endorsed my recommendation that no action should be taken that did not leave the rent freeze basically intact.

That appeared to be that, until one day there appeared on my desk a draft statutory instrument amending the rent freeze. Anthony Crosland, appealed to, ruled that the order could go ahead provided it had my agreement, but not otherwise. Officials appeared in my room for a meeting as if by magic, offering persua-sive reasons why landlords should be compensated for heating costs in midsummer. Only when I told them that, though they could draft as many orders as they liked, I would not rise in my place in the House of Commons to move approval of any of them, did they disperse in puzzled disgruntlement.

Fulfilment of election pledges, you will therefore discover, has its pitfalls. But you will also find out that much of the policy you carry out has nothing at all to do with the fulfilment of election pledges, though you will do your best to frame it in accordance with your party's political principles. Sudden unexpected crises arise which require the immediate response of government. Such, for example, was the collapse of Rolls-Royce in 1971 which led Edward Heath's government – not exactly in line with its expressed Tory principles – to carry out the fastest act of nationalization on record: seventeen hours flat out through both Houses of Parliament. Such, again, was the collapse of British Leyland in 1975, which led the Labour government to implement a similar act of nationalization, a little more slowly but with a good deal more enthusiasm. Later in 1975 came the collapse of Chrysler UK, which again called for urgent government action, though this time wisely not involving encumbering the taxpayer with a dubious asset.

When I was on the staff at Number Ten I remember the Prime Minister's Personal Secretary asking Harold Wilson one day: 'What do ministers *do* with their time all day?' to which he replied, closing the subject: 'They hold meetings.' And you will find that this is indeed what you do a great deal of the time.

What is important is to ensure that these meetings are productive. This means that they must come to conclusions; and this in turn means that they must not go on too long, since every meeting has its point of no return beyond which nothing useful can be achieved and, indeed, what has been achieved can be dissipated. Anthony Crosland had a firm and praiseworthy rule that no meeting in any circumstances should go on for longer than an hour and a half. One minister I knew was not aware of this sage ruling, or regarded it as unsuitable to his own circumstances, allowing meetings to continue for three hours and upwards, at the end of which he was lively and ready for more while all around him officials sat glazed and glancing at their watches, no longer bothering to do so covertly.

The rule is to decide what you want the outcome of the meeting to be, and to work your way steadily towards that conclusion, profiting along the way from the wisdom represented around the table. It is important, too, to set a deadline for the action decided upon – two weeks is always a good limit – with a report-back meeting fixed to ensure that the action is indeed accomplished. Whenever possible you should limit representation at the meeting to officials of your own department, who have to answer to you if they fail to deliver. Officials from other departments have the escape route of appeal to their own minister, together with a rather irritating tendency to plead other work relevant to their own speciality to which they will, if not prevented, give priority.

You will find, therefore, that the swiftest, most satisfying, most reliable kind of policy-making in which you are involved is administrative action which does not require any reference to Parliament, does not have to be remitted for collective decision by ministers, does not affect the interests of any other department and, if at all possible, does not involve any expenditure of money, thus eliminating the involvement of the Treasury.

The Treasury, while full of money, prefers if possible to spend none of it. Many a small, worthwhile plan has been stifled by Treasury reluctance to spend, and this ingenious department will even stoop to pretending that plans which have been collectively agreed must be reconsidered because financial responsibility has not been allocated when it most certainly has. They love to set different departments squabbling as to who will pay for something, a deliberate stirring-up of departmentalitis since, in the end, all the money comes from the taxpayer by way of the Treasury itself. There will be weary references to the intolerable burden on the Contingencies Fund, a mysterious crock of gold which all departments wish to tap, but which Treasury Ministers defend with a vehemence bordering on obsession. Indeed, they wish to add to it by selling off various assets. Treasury costings when carried to extremes bear little relation to real life, as was illustrated by a letter sent to the Department of Industry in 1979 by Sir Douglas Wass, Permanent Secretary at the Treasury, purporting on a narrow accounting basis to evaluate various important industrial projects. The letter was rejected by officials at the Department of Industry and repudiated by Treasury ministers, but did illustrate certain unworldly facets in the minds of these essentially worldly potentates. If you are a Labour minister you will be somewhat puzzled by their proposals to sell off certain very valuable public assets which can be relied on to make long-term gains for the taxpayer, in order to cover a fraction of current debts; of course, if you are a Conservative you will seize upon them and only afterwards have cause for regret.

All the time, then, you are making policy, sometimes successfully, sometimes imperfectly, sometimes inadvertently. Every small action you take is yet another element going to make up what will one day be regarded by historians as the record of the government in which you are a minister. Since you are a loyal and long-standing member of your party you will do your best to ensure that your actions are in accordance with its principles and policies. But sometimes you will be hard put to it to see the connection; and if you cannot, what will activists in the country be likely to think? One minister, barred by Harold Wilson from making a public speech seeking to vindicate his role in a controversy which was dividing the party, wailed to the Prime Minister: 'But I have to justify my actions to my constituents!' To which Harold Wilson witheringly replied: 'In the last election you never got nearer to your constituents than the local golf club.' This minister was an exception. Most others do really care. One day, during what seemed to me a particularly sterile discussion at the Department of Industry, I was unable to stifle the lament: 'What would the members of the General Management Committee of the Ardwick Constituency Labour Party think if they heard all this?' a remark which caused a certain consternation among officials, some of whom were unaware of the existence of any such body.

However, I feel on reflection that I was underestimating the members of the Ardwick GMC. If faced with the never-ceasing difficulties that you have to contend with as a minister, your constituency activists will very likely react in the same way as you do. The snag is that they do not have to face these problems, and can only see the outcome of your actions. Because of this they will tend to regard as a temporizing excuse your explanations of the day-to-day problems of being in government, and the difference between slogans and action. At your most hard pressed you may regard this as unfair. But remember their point of view too. They have reposed a great deal of hope and faith in the government they have worked to elect, and they feel they have a right to see at any rate some of their dreams fulfilled.

6

How to Draft

Making policy is all very well. You will not, however, feel that you have really come of age as a minister until you have participated in the drafting of a Bill, or at the very least of a White Paper. That is not, of course, to decry Green Papers, which have the great merit of fending Parliament off for a time while you try to think of what you actually want to do about some particularly intractable problem.

A Bill, though, is really something. There it is, itself printed on rather greenish paper, with your own name on the cover (together with those of some of your ministerial colleagues, their titles, apparently, plucked out of a bran-tub kept for the purpose in a cellar at the Cabinet Office) and opening with grand rolling words about being enacted by the Queen's most Excellent Majesty, by and with the advice and consent of the Lords Spiritual and Temporal, and Commons, in this present Parliament assembled. It then goes on from there to lay down the new regulations enforcing minimum sizes for cattle grids.

You do not, in fact, have to be a minister to introduce a Bill in Parliament. Any MP or peer can do it, and large numbers do. A ballot is held to give priority to Members of Parliament who wish to introduce their own legislation. Since Bills are very complicated to draft, outside interests will often offer drafted Bills to MPs to introduce. Other members will have their own sometimes very good ideas for legislation but encounter technical difficulties in compiling them. Tom King's Bill to give better protection to occupants of mobile homes, while entirely his own idea, was largely written by civil servants at the Department of the Environment acting on my instructions. Some MPs present Bills, perfectly permissibly, without even making a speech, but just lurk behind the Speaker's chair while the Clerk reads out the title. Some used to introduce Bills on the strength of the title alone, without having an actual Bill written out at all. An unusual MP called Anthony Steen, who was greatly preoccupied with youth clubs and creating enterprise zones in derelict areas of cities, was much given to this, until it became too noticeable and the Speaker put a stop to it. The only explanation for his having persisted in this course of action for such a long time was that he had the right to make a ten-minute speech every time he did it. However, the speech always seemed to be the same, and one theory was that he wanted to go on practising it until he got it right.

There are two major differences, however, between a Private Member's Bill and a Government Bill. The first is that a Private Member's Bill cannot spend money unless authorized in a Money Resolution (of which more later). The second is that a Private Member's Bill has to take its somewhat hazardous chance in Parliament, while a Government Bill is almost certain to be enacted. I say 'almost certain', because there can be pitfalls. Michael Heseltine, as Secretary of State for the Environment, introduced into Parliament at the end of 1979 a Local Government, Planning and Land Bill so immense that it caused controversy as to whether it was eight Bills in one or only five. Be that as it may, it never became law in its intended form, because the government made the error of introducing the Bill in the House of Lords. This action aroused a tremendous uproar, the Opposition maintaining that the government were violating various constitutional conventions which they were perfectly ready to enumerate. The government therefore retired, hurt, to review the situation and, since their legislative timetable was in any case grievously overloaded, withdrew the Bill as originally drafted and a little later introduced a much truncated version in the Commons.

The Labour governments of 1966 and 1974 each similarly miscalculated the reaction of Parliament to legislation they wished to have enacted, and failed to carry Bills which, respectively, sought to reform the House of Lords and introduce devolution for Scotland and Wales. In the latter case, further separate Bills were subsequently introduced and carried. Since one of them led, however, to the downfall of the Labour government, it was not exactly a happy experience.

However, provided you are not over-ambitious, if you are a minister you can look forward with reasonable confidence to your Bill reaching the statute book. The first question is, what is it to be about? Do not ask this question of your civil servants, for they will immediately reach into their desks and produce ideas for Bills which the department has had ready for years. Disregard all such suggestions, since no good can come from them. On one occasion I was due to introduce into the House of Commons a Bill to increase by several billion pounds the amount of money that the British Steel Corporation was allowed to borrow from the government. Despite all the billions it was a very short Bill, and I therefore nodded my casual agreement when officials asked if they could add another clause providing for a technical adjustment to BSC's accounting procedures. It was a serious mistake. The Standing Committee considering the legislation agreed with little ado to the billions of pounds, but then proceeded to get its teeth into the technical change in accounting procedures. It was a wearing experience, and taught me a lesson I never forgot: put nothing into your bill that you do not absolutely need; it simply is not worth the trouble.

So do not look to your civil servants for ideas for your Bill. Look instead to your party's election programme. There will be plenty of inspiration there. And when you have got your legislation through you will be able to reel off the list of manifesto commitments that you personally have fulfilled. Every minister in every government is ready to do this at the drop of a hat and it can prove very tedious, as I have found out by noting that people tend to yawn or even turn away when I try it.

The simplest kind of Bills are non-controversial Bills. When the Conservatives lost office in 1974 they had ready for introduction a Housing Bill which made various desirable changes in the law relating to house improvements and housing associations. The incoming Labour government took it over, rewrote it a little, and got it through Parliament. By coincidence the Labour government that fell in 1979 also had a Housing Bill of a non-partisan character ready and the incoming Conservative government, in their turn, adopted large parts of it and inserted them as a non-controversial core into their very controversial Bill for the compulsory sale of council houses.

Having decided what your Bill is to be about, you will next want to make up your mind as to precisely what to put in it. The ideal, as I have pointed out, is to keep it as short as possible. The longer it is, the more it will provoke opposition, and the longer it will take to get through Parliament. So you will put in the minimum possible of content. In the case of the steel industry when it was in public ownership, this was very simple. You simply put in large sums of money. All this needed was the agreement of the Treasury.

All legislation going forward in your name will originate inside your own department. Officials will put up a submission to ministers, which will then be either approved or discussed. In the case of a Bill introduced in 1978 to provide statutory redundancy payments for workers who lost their jobs in the shipbuilding industry, officials at first recommended that the payments should go only to workers actually engaged in shipbuilding itself. Ministers found this unsatisfactory, since they were aware that the jobs of many workers engaged in shiprepair were also in danger. Officials, however, pointed out that while almost all shipbuilding workers were employed by the nationalized British Shipbuilders, about half the shiprepair workers were employed by private enterprise firms. After consideration, it was felt that it was wrong for the taxpayer to be expected to fund payments which were the responsibility of a private employer. Ministers, rather ingeniously, they felt, then came up with the solution that the payments should go to all employees of subsidiary companies owned by British Shipbuilders who were made redundant. Officials smartly countered by pointing out that the employees of British Shipbuilders subsidiaries included, because of the rag-bag of companies taken into state ownership by the nationalization act, some workers engaged in housebuilding and quarrying, who could scarcely be regarded as casualties of the world shipping slump. The ministerial solution was therefore adopted in principle, with certain agreed exceptions.

Once the basic policy issues of your Bill have been settled within your department, you take them to the appropriate Cabinet Committee for collective agreement. But when you obtain policy approval, as you generally do, that is far from the end of the story. Indeed, that is when the real work begins. First you have to agree all the financial details with the Treasury, one of whose ministers will have his name appended to the Bill as a sign of monetary rectitude. Then you have to consult with outside interests which are likely to be affected by the legislation. Some departments do this by issuing consultative documents. Michael Heseltine really got into the spirit of things in connection with his 1979 Housing Bill, giving the impression that all his life he had been labouring under a compulsion, now at last released, to send out endless chain-letters. Most consultation, however, will be more limited.

In the case of shipbuilding redundancy payments, for example, the employers (British Shipbuilders) and the workers' representatives (the Confederation of Shipbuilding and Engineering Unions) were asked to go away and work out the scheme themselves, having been told the rough financial parameters and having also been warned of the dangers of Repercussions. Repercussions, which were a source of constant preoccupation during Labour's initially successful but eventually ill-fated non-statutory pay policy, mean that what is gained by one group of workers will be demanded by another. It is therefore necessary to place limits on what can be offered to the group with whom you are dealing, because every other union will be watching the proceedings with absorbed interest. British Shipbuilders and the Confederation therefore conducted their own consultations, went away, and after a time came back with an agreed scheme. Most of it was acceptable to the government, although parts were not. It was therefore possible after further discussion to proceed with an enabling bill, to be followed by regulations embodying the actual scheme.

The sadly short-lived experiment in industrial democracy in the Post Office provided a more complicated consultative procedure. Here again the Post Office Board (reluctant but compliant) and the Council of Post Office Unions (enthusiastic) were invited at a specially convened conference, at which I was chairman, to work out a scheme for worker representation in Post Office management which, if acceptable, the government would authorize. Snags were encountered along the way, but eventually an agreed plan was produced, allowing for an equal number of management and union representatives on the main Post Office Board balanced by a group of independent board members. This formula, however, required an increase in the size of the Post Office Board, and legislation was therefore needed.

Since the Labour government had meanwhile lost its majority in Parliament, the Cabinet decided that the project could only go ahead if the enabling legislation was assured of a majority in the Commons. I was therefore instructed to seek to construct such a majority by conducting negotiations for support from all the non-Conservative opposition parties in Parliament. I met them all, from the Ulster Unionists through to the Liberals. I was told later, with what truth I am not sure, that it was this exercise in consultation that gave David Steel the idea for the Lib-Lab pact. The Lib-Lab pact did indeed follow before the Bill had been introduced and under the terms of the pact I had to conduct a fresh set of negotiations, this time with the Liberals alone. They insisted that the independent members of the board should include spokesmen for the Post Office users, and, after a certain amount of haggling, this was agreed. The legislation was therefore authorized, and went through Parliament in a matter of hours. After the seemingly endless negotiations, no one voted against it at any stage.

When plans for legislation have made the necessary progress, the Leader of the House authorizes that drafting should proceed. This involves giving instructions to Parliamentary Counsel. Parliamentary Counsel are a closed shop of specialist lawyers, who live in what I am convinced is an attic in obscure premises at the less fashionable end of Whitehall. Only they, we are assured, have the knack of drafting Bills, though even they, as we shall see, are capable of making mistakes. However, even these paragons require to be given instructions. And a meeting for the purpose of formulating these is convened in the department originating the legislation.

You will recall that the prime desideratum is that the Bill should be as short and uncomplicated as possible. It should also be devised to ensure as easy a parliamentary passage as can be contrived. The 1979 Industry Bill was a measure designed to increase the borrowing limits of the National Enterprise Board (a publicly funded body which provided financial aid for selected companies) together with the Scottish and Welsh Development Agencies. It had not escaped our notice that a Bill with this multiple purpose would be likely to secure an easier passage, since it would have the support of the Scottish and Welsh National Parties, then a formidable group fourteen strong. The draftsmen took the view that there should be a separate clause for each agency. It seemed to me, however, that the best way of getting the Bill through was to entangle the financial provision for all three agencies to such an extent that the nationalist parties would have no option but to vote for the whole Bill. I therefore said that I would like the Bill drafted certainly in one clause, and if possible in one sentence. The draftsmen exclaimed in horror at the technical impossibility of such a task, and then went away and did it with great skill.

Once you have your Bill drafted, it goes to the Legislation Committee of the Cabinet, where it is examined with special care by the Attorney-General in particular. The Legislation Committee decides whether the Bill should be given priority for introduction in Parliament. If you get the green light for this, you breathe a sigh of relief; you are on your way. A day is set for introduction; the bran-tub is rummaged in for the names of sponsors. And one day the Order Paper of the House of Commons contains the notice of introduction. You hurry along to your place on the front bench and at 3.30 p.m. the Clerk reads out (for example): 'Shipbuilding Redundancy Payments Bill'. You then Nod. Your Nod means that the Bill has received its First Reading. The Speaker then calls out, 'Second Reading what day?' The Whip on the Bench (who knows exactly what to say because it is all written down in a loose-leaf booklet, the bible of the Whips' Bench, entitled 'Useful Cries') calls out: 'Tomorrow, Sir'. This means that the Bill will *not* have its Second Reading tomorrow, but this is a Parliamentary tradition shrouded in the mists of antiquity, and must be gone through. You may then leave the front bench and return to your department to consider another submission from Mr Dearing. The Bill has been launched.

Your Bill may have been preceded by a White Paper setting out the broad principles of the legislation to follow. But White Papers need not necessarily propose legislation at all. They can simply be a broad (or detailed) statement of government policy on some important issue. Departments have quite a predilection for issuing them.

Be warned. Make sure it is your White Paper. Otherwise the sheer pace of events may sweep you along into proposing notions with which you do not really agree. Given half a chance your departmental officials, who are beavers for work whatever their other qualities, will go away and write the entire White Paper and then, with smug smiles, send up to you the completed draft accompanied, of course, by a submission. Barbara Castle and, I believe, Duncan Sandys used to prevent this by sitting down and writing every word of the White Paper themselves. This is, indeed, the best way.

If lack of time and other preoccupations prevent this, you should at the very least start by having a meeting with your officials and tell them both what you do want in the White Paper and, just as important, what you do not want. This is crucial, because he who controls the first draft controls the White Paper. If your officials put up a first draft for your comments and you go on from there, you have lost: the White Paper may be admirable; you may agree with quite a lot of it; but it will have gathered too much momentum to be brought back into control. Moreover, if your officials know what you would like the contents to be, they can think up solutions to difficult problems along the way. This method was, for example, very helpful in compiling the White Paper on the Post Office in 1978. It led to the production of a formula acceptable to many differing interests on the vexed issue of the splitting of the Post Office into separate posts and telecommunications businesses.

When you receive the first draft of the White Paper you should take it home with you, sit over a glass of brandy with it, and rewrite it. You should start with an introduction which will set the mood for the whole document, and which you should write entirely yourself. You should then go through the rest of it word by word, remembering that not only will this be accepted as an authoritative statement of government policy, but that it will stand as such possibly for years to come. Take especial account of the possibility that you may lose the next election and that the Opposition, by then the government, will seek if at all possible to use the document against you. It was all these considerations which governed my attitude to the 1978 White Paper on the steel industry, *The Road to Viability*, which was accepted by all interests at the time of publication and which the 1979 Conservative government, during the assault on the British Steel Corporation which it launched in late 1979 (a prelude to the removal of the BSC from the state sector in 1988), was unable to use against the former Labour government, dearly as it would have liked to do so.

White Papers in response to reports of Select Committees are a species all of their own. Whenever a Select Committee of the House of Commons issues a report, the relevant department or departments are required to compile a White Paper or other document responding in detail to the Select Committee's proposals. In 1978 the Select Committee on Nationalized Industries (a body which later had its throat cut by the Conservative government) issued a series of reports on the British Steel Corporation, one of which was, among other matters, severely critical of myself. That aspect was dealt with in a parliamentary debate, in which to my relief I was happily vindicated by a large majority. But I felt in consequence that it was especially important that this committee's recommendations should be considered with particular care, and the government accepted several of them. This, among other things, should warn you of the great power of Parliamentary Select Committees should they choose to exercise it.

Whatever the reason for your White Paper, it has to be submitted to the Cabinet, which will solemnly go through it page by page. It is, after all, a statement of policy for the whole government, though some of your colleagues may later protest that they did not notice at the time and that the whole matter is a terrible shock to them. It will then be laid before Parliament. If it is very important indeed, like the annual Public Expenditure White Paper, it will be debated very quickly. The inability of the Labour government to muster a majority for its Expenditure White Paper in 1977 led directly to a vote of no confidence and to the Lib-Lab pact. If the White Paper is somewhat less important, it may never be debated at all, although members preoccupied with that particular issue will rise regularly every Thursday afternoon and call on the Leader of the House to provide time for it to be discussed. His invariable reply will be, 'Not next week'. That, to all intents and purposes, will be the end of the active life of the White Paper on which you have laboured so devotedly. But your work will not have been in vain. The White Paper will be there to be studied by all who afterwards take an interest in the area of policy that it covers. It may even provide them with enlightenment.

7

How to Get On in Cabinet Committee

Only Cabinet ministers attend Cabinet meetings as of right, although the Chief Whip is invited to all of them. Junior ministers are sometimes called in for individual items. They wait nervously, in the reception area outside the Cabinet Room at Number Ten, until a head pops round the door and summons them inside. You cannot of course rely on starting out your career in government as a Cabinet minister (though if you faithfully follow all the advice in this manual you will assuredly eventually become one). But whatever the station in ministerial life to which the Prime Minister has called you, you will undoubtedly attend meetings of Cabinet Committees. That is an understatement; you will probably attend hundreds. Every one of them is technically a Cabinet meeting, and all the decisions reached at them are fully fledged Cabinet decisions; although it is open to a department dissatisfied with a Cabinet Committee decision to seek to take it to Cabinet for reconsideration this is rarely done. The Prime Minister controls the Cabinet agenda and he understandably does not like meetings of the full Cabinet to be cluttered up with left-overs from Committees which are set up in the first place to keep the Cabinet agenda clear for the most important issues.

The Prime Minister decides what are to be the Cabinet Committees which will have a regular and continuing existence. There will be certain major ones dealing with key areas of policy, of which he himself will take the chair; there will be others whose chairmen will be other senior Cabinet ministers whom the Prime Minister will select. All of these Committees will have as their titles baffling combinations of initials, almost like a code. From time to time the Prime Minister will also set up temporary Cabinet Committees, which will consider and report on specific and urgent policy issues and then be disbanded; these are known as MISCS or GENS (the titles alternate between successive Prime Ministers) with a distinguishing number after the MISC or the GEN. The MISCS (MISCellaneous?) or the GENS (GENeral?) can be manned by a mixture of ministers and officials, or be simply committees of officials perhaps presided over by a minister, who again is selected by the Prime Minister. All their activities, however, are Cabinet proceedings. In my time I was nominated to preside over three GENS and since one coincided with Christmas, I interrupted the proceedings for festive drinks which, in my droll way, I described as GEN and tonic. The membership of all Cabinet Committees is decided by the Prime Minister. Other departments, not represented, get to hear of the subjects to be discussed. If they feel that their departmental interests are affected they can seek permission – not invariably granted – to attend. When granted permission they have an equal voice with everyone else present.

You should take careful note that Cabinet, including Cabinet Committees, has absolute priority over all other ministerial activities except attendance in Parliament to speak for your department. Do not imagine that you can get out of a Cabinet Committee by pleading an urgent constituency engagement or indeed anything except debilitating illness. You are not even forgiven for being late. Timings are decided by the Cabinet Office, who have the fiendish task of fitting Cabinet Committee meetings into the already crowded timetables of dozens of ministers. The nearest they will get to accommodating your own personal requirements is to advise the Committee chairman that you would like a particular item to be placed early on the agenda.

If you are the minister scheduled to attend the meeting in question (for some Committees the Prime Minister will only allow the head of the designated department to attend, at others he will allow substitutions) you will have had circulated to you before the meeting an agenda, together with the papers submitted by departments which are seeking a decision from their colleagues. All papers have to be circulated at least forty-eight hours before the meeting, and the Treasury have to have an advance view of all papers involving expenditure so that, if they wish, they can put in a paper of their own. Other departments can submit a paper if they wish and some often do.

Before the meeting itself you will receive the departmental

briefing. The whole collection of papers will be enclosed in a handsome folder handed to you before you leave for the meeting by your Private Secretary. You should do your best not to lose it, since everything in it is Confidential, at very least. Your departmental briefing documents are works of art. They will analyse the issue in question and the papers concerned, not from the standpoint of the government as a whole but purely from the departmental point of view. They will advise you on the 'Line to Take' (a heading all on its own), the sentences beginning with masterly injunctions such as, 'The minister will wish to say . . .' (This form of words was, in fact, banished from all briefing documents submitted to me but officials, nothing abashed, simply submitted alternative formulations which amounted to the same thing.) They will even include speaking notes, which the minister can read out without having taken the trouble to study the actual Cabinet papers at all. This did indeed happen from time to time at meetings I attended, the minister in question giving himself away by unusual fluency and cogency of argument, coupled with stumbles over faulty punctuation. Other ministers would hide smiles of amused superiority but at one meeting, dealing with an exceptionally complicated subject, all those gathered together simply read out their briefs to each other; it seemed the most sensible thing to do.

There is no need, of course, for you to pay any attention whatever to these briefs. All you really have to do is to read the Cabinet papers, seek from your department any further information you need, and make up your own mind, assuming of course that your opinion is not contrary to that of your Secretary of State. You can even listen to the discussion at the meeting, and make up your mind on the basis of that. In the Labour government some ministers, such as Edmund Dell and Peter Shore, were notorious for doing this and were consequently branded as simultaneously brilliant and unreliable.

The day for the meeting will come and you will arrive at the meeting place. When Parliament is not sitting, or when there is no Parliamentary Whip, the meetings will be held at the Cabinet Office at 70 Whitehall, where there is a positive warren of Conference Rooms; during busy parliamentary sittings the meetings will take place in ministerial Conference Rooms situated directly below the House of Commons Chamber itself. If the meeting is held at the Cabinet Office you will, as you go in, be vetted and ticked off from a list by custodians who, when I went there for Cabinet Committees only, seemed to be very authoritarian but who, when I saw them a great deal more often during my spell working in the Cabinet Office, turned out to be really quite homely. You can always tell when a Cabinet Committee is taking place at the Cabinet Office, even when you are not involved yourself, since the kerb outside is lined with ministerial cars (these days mainly Rovers, but with occasional Ford Mondeos and Vauxhall Vectras to which lower-ranking ministers may be consigned).

When you enter the designated Conference Room you will find the table bordered with cardboard name plates indicating where everyone should sit. These are distributed in exact order of hierarchy, which the Cabinet Office have brought to a fine art. Before each place will be a notepad and pencil, useful for sending notes. The chairman will open the proceedings, the minister with the first paper on the agenda will introduce it, and the discussion will begin. The chairman will have a steering brief provided by the Cabinet Office and, if he strays too much from it, the member of the Cabinet Office staff who is sitting beside him taking a meticulous and immaculate note will murmur in his ear. As at Cabinet meetings, no vote is taken, but the chairman gathers the voices in his summing-up. The summing-up is the key event. It embodies the decision of the Cabinet on the issue in question and serves as an inflexible instruction to the ministers concerned. This in its turn is embodied in the Cabinet minute circulated to all concerned immediately afterwards. The minute is phrased in courteous language – 'The Minister of State, Department of Industry, was invited to . . .' – but the instruction is firm, if not brutal. It is confirmed by the indented statement that the Committee noted 'with approval' the chairman's summing-up. Cabinet minutes are studied in government departments with the reverence generally reserved for sacred texts, and can be triumphantly produced conclusively to settle any argument. Departments await the outcome of these meetings with such anxiety that when they end the Cabinet Office telephone lines are hot with incoming calls.

Some of the items considered will be issues for which precedent requires collective decision. Others will go there because you have had a difference of opinion with the Treasury which you are seeking the assistance of others to resolve. Some matters will have been the subject of correspondence between yourself and groups of ministerial colleagues. Cabinet Office likes as many problems as possible to be settled that way, since it leaves the actual Committee agenda less congested; but if even one minister refuses to agree to a decision which others in correspondence have accepted, then the matter finds its way on to the agenda of a Cabinet Committee.

In the course of your ministerial life you will take dozens of issues to Cabinet Committees. If you consistently win, you will be thought of highly in your department. If you lose, you yourself may take it to heart but your officials, being adaptable and realistic, will immediately change tack and accept the new policy. I remember how amazed I was, after the most bruising of all such episodes I went through, that while I brooded over it and could not be reconciled to the outcome – almost, but not quite, to the extent of resigning – the departmental officials who had urged me on accepted the decision instantly and got on placidly with something else.

However, if at all possible you want to win. This is not simply a matter of prestige. You may feel really passionately on the subject. Alan Williams, my fellow Minister of State at the Department of Industry, fought like a tiger to win parliamentary time for his Bill setting up a Co-operative Development Agency. His colleagues at the relevant Committee were so impressed with his eloquence (which gained added strength from the Prime Minister's personal sponsorship of the project) that, though the timetable was crammed to over-capacity and every other department was jostling for a place in it, they gave way to his importunings.

You must start by making sure that the Cabinet Paper you are to submit is compellingly argued. This means that, as with a White Paper, you should either write it yourself or give detailed instructions on how it is to be drafted. This is no idle advice. On one important issue that I was preparing to take to Cabinet Committee, on which I was in contention with the Treasury, I read with amazement the first draft which had been submitted to me of 'my' Cabinet Paper. It was entirely contrary to my own wishes and, when questioned, officials bashfully admitted that it had been drafted in the Treasury itself. The final version was better, and I won with it.

In compiling a Cabinet Paper you must do your best to square all other departments which will be represented at the meeting, so that if possible they can let your paper through with little or no opposition. This is where you bring your officials into play. It is their job to contact their counterparts in the other departments who will be preparing the briefing for their own ministers. If you can get the other ministers at the Committee briefed in your favour, the battle is nearly over. But take into account that your own officials may oppose you and may, if they have failed to get their way within your department, indeed be stirring up the opposition in other departments rather than pacifying it. The acme of this particular approach occurred so far as I was concerned when, reading my departmental briefing on an issue which I was taking to a Cabinet Committee, I discovered to my bemusement that my officials were briefing me to oppose my own proposal. I took care to win on that one as well.

If you cannot get your officials to disarm the opposition, then there is only one thing for it. You will have to resort to your own most basic political technique – and canvass. On one occasion I was in contention with the Treasury about two items of expenditure for which I was anxious to obtain authorization: funding to continue a holding contract on a projected small civil aircraft then known as the HS146 and additional funding for an ageing but still sturdy plane, the BAC 1-11. My department approved of the BAC 1-11, but not of the HS146. Officials came to me with great satisfaction, telling me that they had gained Treasury approval for the item they favoured though not for the other, and advising me to accept my partial victory and let the matter rest. I did not want to do this.

I therefore sought a meeting with Joel Barnett, the appropriate Treasury minister, and, since he was senior in the pecking order, went along to his office to bargain with him. Both of the items in question cost roughly the same amount of money, and I offered to abandon the one he had accepted if he would grant me instead the one he had rejected. I thought this reasonable, and he considered it with care; but in the end he turned me down. Again, my officials advised me to accept the situation. But I refused, and decided to take the issue to Cabinet Committee.

I acquired a list of all the members of it, including even such rare attenders as the Chief Whip, and went round them all pleading for my cause. The result was that, when the Committee met, I received overwhelming support not only for the item to which I gave priority but for both items. It happened that we were meeting in a ministerial Conference Room in the House of Commons, immediately prior to a speech I had to make in the Chamber on the very subject in question. I therefore sought and received permission to announce right away in the House the decision we had just reached. I dashed out of the Committee, ran up the stairs to my officials waiting for me behind the Speaker's Chair, told them of what had happened, and then went into the Chamber and made the announcement. The subject was pretty contentious in party political terms, and I spoke amid mounting uproar from the Opposition. When I came to this particular announcement Nicholas Winterton, a Conservative MP who had spent his years in Parliament successfully concealing his squeamish aversion to political controversy, called out furiously: 'This is a Labour Party political broadcast.' He did not know how near I had come to not being able to make the announcement at all. The HS146, later renamed the BAe146 when Hawker Siddeley Aviation was merged into the nationalized British Aerospace, was eventually built, became a considerable success, and is now flown by airlines throughout the world, a telling testimonial to the Treasury's legendary perspicacity.

You will enjoy these heady moments of triumph. But do not grow over-confident. I did and, failing to take the necessary precautions, at a subsequent meeting of the same Committee was defeated – as crushingly as I had previously been successful – on a proposal for expenditure less than one-twentieth in magnitude of that on which I had won so triumphantly.

In Cabinet Committee your reputation is at stake every time you open your mouth. Your colleagues will judge your quality by your performance there more than by your achievements on the floor of the House, which in any case they will be unlikely to be present to witness, preoccupied as they are by their own departmental duties. No one will pull rank on you in Cabinet Committee. You may be there as a Parliamentary Secretary surrounded by senior Cabinet ministers, but they will judge you not by your seniority but by the quality of your argument. Similarly, they will have no mercy on you just because you are junior. It is a meeting of equals.

Do not go unprepared. If you are presenting a paper, the chairman will question you as if he were prosecuting you. Edward

Short, when Leader of the House of Commons, was as relentless as his experience as a former headmaster could make him. But the most difficult of all to satisfy were the two Prime Ministers under whom I served, Harold Wilson and James Callaghan. Both were masters of the papers under discussion, having clearly studied them in great detail. If dissatisfied they could be devastating. I remember Harold Wilson leaving humiliated a senior Cabinet minister who was forced to admit that he had not himself read a paper for which he was seeking approval. On the other hand, both were very generous when impressed with a performance.

The proceedings at a Cabinet Committee may be casual: a group of men and women gathered round a baize-covered table in a big room in an old house. The procedure may be informal: you may be unsure whether to refer to your neighbour as the Minister of X or just Fred, though you will always address the chairman formally, particularly if he is the Prime Minister. Jokes may be cracked, notes may be passed. But you are deciding really big issues: the future of the steel industry, what is to be done about nuclear power, what should Britain's policy be at a major international conference. You never in your wildest dreams imagined that you would get to such a place. Recognize your privilege and do justice to it.

8

How to Work with Number Ten

———

Your meeting with the Prime Minister is over. You are now a member of Her Majesty's Government. You walk out of the front door of Number Ten and make your way towards your new department. What will your relationship be now with the Prime Minister who has just appointed you? Clearly it cannot be what it was half an hour ago. The man is now not only the head of the government and the Leader of your Party. He is your boss. In addition, he is a man of great power, and that power may be helpful to you in your ministerial duties. How should you take the best advantage of that?

You may not be a member of the Cabinet, who sees him regularly and gets to know his mind fairly intimately. But it is important for you to know the way his mind is working, since that will be the tone he sets for his government, a tone which you will either accept – or reject, in which case after a time you will no longer wish to be a member of his government and will resign. You should therefore as one of your first acts instruct your Diary Secretary to put Prime Minister's Question Time – 3.15 to 3.30 p.m. every Tuesday and Thursday when Parliament is sitting – as a permanent engagement in your diary. You should also do your best to attend all the major debates in which the Prime Minister speaks (as well as other major debates; you are a Member of Parliament as well as a minister).

While you need to take a close interest in what the Prime Minister says and does, do not imagine that he will in return be watching everything you do. Some ministers do seem to believe this. They get the notion that every speech they deliver, every slip they make or every small success they notch up, is somehow being noted by the Prime Minister ready for a grand end-of-term report. While, as we shall see, he is not unaware of your activities, do not be foolish enough to believe that he is keeping a close check on your every move. For one thing, he has given you a job to do and simply expects you to get on with it. Secondly, he simply does not have the time.

Apart from Cabinet itself and Cabinet Committees he has a daunting number of meetings to attend. These include, if he is a Labour Prime Minister, meetings of the party's National Executive Committee, of which he is ex officio (as leader of the Party, not as Prime Minister) a member, with a voice and vote equal to that of the representative of the Labour Clubs. He will need to ensure that the links between the party and the government are kept as strong as possible, since otherwise there will be disaffection in the constituencies and difficulties at the annual conference. He will have public meetings to address, and will always attend the meetings of the Parliamentary Labour Party in order to keep in touch with the mood among his MPs. (This is not so with a Conservative Prime Minister who, like his ministers, can only attend meetings of the back bench 1922 Committee by invitation.) He alone among ministers is in automatic receipt of the papers and minutes of all Cabinet Committees, which he will study with care as a check on what is going on, and a focus on possible danger points. Sometimes, in addition, chairmen of Cabinet Committees will write to him reporting on certain important decisions or failures to agree. He has factories to tour, old people's homes to visit, conferences abroad to attend, and weekly audiences with the Queen. He is quite busy enough without needing to be bothered about you.

But, you will whine, he would certainly pay attention to my important activities if I were one of his cronies. Ever since Harold Wilson dubbed Harold Macmillan's administration 'Government by crony', cronyism has been a dirty word in British public life. You will be surprised to find that the Prime Minister is unlikely to have any cronies, if you define such people as those who have access to him whenever they wish. Of course he has colleagues who were close to him in the past, ex-Parliamentary Private Secretaries, for example. But they will find that – and, to incredulous colleagues, will protest that – they now see little of him. They certainly cannot expect any special favours from him. When James Callaghan became Prime Minister almost all those who had been intimately involved with him in the past were already members of the Labour government – put there by Harold Wilson on their merits. He failed on taking office to promote a single one of them, unless you include as promotion the advancement of one Minister of State from junior to senior rank. His Parliamentary Private Secretary, John Cunningham, had to wait several months for inclusion in the government, and then only at Under-Secretary of State level.

On the other hand, while Callaghan refused to single out his friends for favour, he did give advancement to members of the left-wing Tribune Group who had most keenly supported Michael Foot, his opponent in the leadership election which made him Prime Minister. Albert Booth and Stanley Orme were promoted to the Cabinet, and junior posts were offered to Robert Cryer and Leslie Huckfield (accepted) and Neil Kinnock and Norman Atkinson (rejected). He did this for the simple and sensible purpose of maintaining a proper balance of party views in his administration. Callaghan reserved his most spectacular promotion, to the Foreign Secretaryship, for David Owen, a junior minister who had voted against him in the leadership election, first in favour of Roy Jenkins, then for Denis Healey.

Harold Wilson, too, gave disproportionate favour to Roy Jenkins's supporters, a perverse action on his part since not only did he continue to think of himself as of the left in the Labour Party (support by the left had been the core of the vote which elected him Party Leader in 1963) but he was particularly distrustful of the approach to Labour politics of Roy Jenkins himself. However, he too saw the need for a balanced government, and he respected the talents of many of Jenkins's admirers. Harold Wilson started off David Owen's ministerial career, appointing him when he was only thirty. Wilson indeed made it clear when he was elected leader that, since it would be invidious for him to have social relationships with some of his MPs and not others, he would have social relationships with none of them. This was no great loss to him (nor perhaps to them) since he had never been a social animal.

You may feel that even though the Prime Minister is not blatantly favouring his old friends over you, your democratic rights as a Member of Parliament and minister are being usurped by an undemocratically selected Kitchen Cabinet. Do not be too easily taken in. There is no evidence whatever that James Callaghan was the centre of such a body. His closest associates were Tom McCaffrey, a career civil servant who went with him from the Foreign

Office to Number Ten and accompanied him into Opposition when the 1979 election was lost, and Tom McNally, a former Transport House employee who occupied Marcia Williams's old office in Number Ten adjoining the Cabinet Room and as she did acted as an outspoken political adviser. Tom McNally entered Parliament in 1979, but no thanks to any intervention by James Callaghan (even if that would have helped McNally in a distrustfully anti-Establishment Labour Party). Indeed, the Prime Minister was somewhat disgruntled at his aide's decision to launch out on his own (as Harold Wilson was with mine), though not so disgruntled as when McNally eventually launched himself out of the Labour Party and into the Social Democratic Party.

Harold Wilson, on the other hand, is firmly believed to have had a Kitchen Cabinet. Certainly he would have had one if wishing could have created one. Richard Crossman ardently desired such a body to exist, with himself as a key member of it. While he could be very critical of Wilson, Crossman deeply admired him too, envying him for what he saw as his almost unique ability to communicate equally effectively with ordinary working people – with whom, himself a provincial detesting metropolitan ways, he instinctively empathized – and high-powered intellectuals. When I first arrived at Number Ten in October 1965 I was invited to join a small group of people who met more or less regularly each week; much flattered, I accepted. I found that I was among such distinguished persons as Crossman himself (then Minister of Housing), Tony Benn (in those days Anthony Wedgwood Benn and Postmaster-General; Benn was an old friend of mine, whom I had in fact consulted before accepting the Downing Street job), Thomas Balogh, Wilson's economic adviser, Peter Shore, Wilson's Parliamentary Private Secretary (who did not attend very regularly since he was much more interested in a book he was writing at the time) and Marcia Williams, his Personal and Political Secretary. While Harold Wilson certainly knew that this group existed, he did not instigate it and was not over-interested in its activities. Nor did he need to be.

We would meet at the home of Crossman, Benn or Balogh for a meal, and there would be a desultory discussion. For me, new to events at the centre of politics, it was enthralling, and I lapped it up. But although attempts were made to discuss various important themes, and to try to find a way of focusing public attention on the achievements of the new and shaky Labour government, the discussion really tended to slide imperceptibly into high-level gossip, with Crossman justifiably crowing over the kind of small triumphs which I have insinuated into this book in the guise of examples, and reporting on his latest row with 'The Dame' (Dame Evelyn Sharp, the Permanent Secretary at the Ministry of Housing). Tony Benn, again with much justice, would cite the latest example of obstructionism by the civil service. Balogh would pursue one of his endearing vendettas.

Few men involved in British public life in recent years have made a more brilliant contribution than Thomas Balogh, though this was at times seriously undervalued – partly through xenophobia, he being a Hungarian by origin. His analysis of our economic problems turned out to be almost totally accurate. A charming and generous man, held in great affection by all close to him, he gave me a special reason for gratitude to him since it was he, I discovered much later, who recommended me for appointment at Number Ten, I believe on the strength of my work for the *New Statesman*. Nevertheless, he could be infuriating.

He tended to appear looming at the door to Marcia Williams's room at Number Ten, and declaim, in his carefully cultivated Hungarian accent, the doomful warning: 'Helsby must go!' Helsby was Sir Laurence Helsby, the head of the civil service, an eminent person who did in fact eventually go, due not to Thomas's vendetta but to his reaching retiring age. At this stage he was elevated to the House of Lords, there to sit not too far from Balogh himself, who was advanced to the peerage an irritating six weeks later than his adversary. When Thomas made his pronouncement, the Prime Minister would say absently, 'Thomas, do stop it,' and go on to talk about something else. I am glad to report that Helsby's departure from Whitehall and Balogh's departure from Downing Street, eventually to join the 1974 Labour government as a first-rate Minister of State at the Department of Energy, by no means put an end to his vendettas. Eric Varley, when Secretary of State there, told me that Balogh conducted a relentless campaign for the removal of one of that department's most senior officials, which in its turn and as inevitably came to nothing.

From time to time Crossman would ask Marcia Williams to

intercede with Harold Wilson for our group to meet him, and occasionally he would agree. Nothing came of these meetings, though they no doubt provided useful relaxation for the Prime Minister among his weightier preoccupations. One of them he was not even able to attend, even though we were meeting over a scratch dinner in the kitchen of his small flat in Downing Street. (I cannot remember whether this was the occasion when I am supposed, as Crossman recalled it, to have eaten Jewish fried eggs, whatever they may be.) Wilson was taking part in a meeting in the Cabinet Room with a foreign dignitary and, since he liked to share his treats, brought his guest up to meet us: a huge, towering figure garbed in flowing robes, the Prime Minister of Nigeria, Alhaji Sir Abubakar Tafawa Balewa. The Alhaji was unfortunately three days later found murdered in a roadside ditch in his native Nigeria. My meetings with Nigerian leaders were often forewarnings of doom since an encounter with General Gowon, whom I encountered at Beating the Retreat in June 1975, only briefly anteceded that diminutive but agreeable person's overthrow.

That was the nearest Wilson got to having a Kitchen Cabinet since, for what it was worth, it did actually meet in his kitchen. In fact, the people who worked for Wilson – Peter Shore and Eric Varley among his Parliamentary Private Secretaries, Thomas Balogh, and Stuart Holland (who was a junior member of the Downing Street staff, later became a highly regarded contributor to the formulation of Labour Party policy and subsequently was, for a time, a highly opinionated Labour MP) were all later to prove themselves as figures of consequence. At the time they were denounced by one journalist as being of low intellectual calibre: sadly, we cannot all be Alfred Shermans and Graham Brights.

Working for Harold Wilson had its ordeals, the worst of these being the hazard from his pipes, with which he would frequently set himself on fire. We would get out of a railway sleeper at 7.30 a.m. (he having slept soundly, which he could do anywhere, while the rest of his party imprisoned on those shuddering vehicles almost certainly had not even closed their eyes) and into the close confinement with him of a cramped old-style Rover. The Prime Minister would immediately light up a pipe containing the uniquely noxious tobacco that he had specially dispatched to him from Scotland, and those enclosed with him would, as Mary Wilson feelingly put it, be 'kippered'. Legend had it that Harold Wilson only smoked a pipe for public display, in private reverting solely to cigars. If only this had been true.

On the other hand he was a most considerate employer, and more receptive to criticism than any other person placed in authority whom I have ever met. He was particularly attentive to views when he was drafting his speeches and did not object, however trenchantly the criticism was expressed. Marcia Williams had grown so used to this, having worked for him for a great many years and being accustomed to say exactly what she thought, that she was astounded to find that all politicians did not react this way. She discovered this when she and I were called in by Richard Crossman – by then the Lord President of the Council – to help with a speech he was writing. Her first minor objection to one of his ideas was greeted with an explosion of rage, which caused her to recoil in terror. Crossman's reaction did not surprise me at all, since I had worked as his assistant for four years at the *Daily Mirror* and knew such a response to be automatic with him prior to his carefully considering and almost invariably accepting the proffered suggestion.

However, working for Harold Wilson, and even being admitted to friendship with his family, did not give one any special privileges. When I first arrived at Number Ten I was denied access to Downing Street notepaper as well as use of the Downing Street telephone switchboard, having to have a special telephone installed, plugged into the House of Commons exchange and paid for by the Labour Party. It was only in my final months that I was allowed to see Cabinet papers of the least confidential kind, which were kept carefully in a box on a ledge in the Number Ten Private Office where I was allowed gingerly to glance at them but under no circumstances to take them out of the room.

In fact in your first day or two as a junior minister you will see more confidential documents than I did during the whole of my five years as an envied member of the Prime Minister's staff. So do not be concerned at the possibility of being excluded from the Prime Minister's counsels in favour of cronies or Kitchen Cabinet members. In any case, the Prime Minister will take care to seek your advice as a minister if he feels he needs it. He may pounce on you in the Division Lobby for a piece of information of which he thinks you may be the unique possessor. He may even second you for a time to a special assignment, as James Callaghan did with me in 1979, calling me into his room in the House of Commons just after I had made the winding-up speech on the Second Reading of the Industry Bill and advising me that until further notice I would be operating not from my department but from the Cabinet Office.

He is quite likely to ask your advice about the most crucial matters. In March 1977, at the very height of the crisis over the Conservative vote of no confidence and with his government's future at stake, James Callaghan was host at a dinner arranged some time before at 10 Downing Street for leading scientists and industrialists. A number of ministers and Members of Parliament were present, myself included, and at the end of the meal and discussion we were asked to remain. There in the pillared room he sat with us and asked our opinions as to whether he should go into a pact with the Liberals, and it was clear that he was deeply anxious to find out what we thought. The most trenchant view of all was that of Tom McNally, maintaining the reputation of occupants of his office for frankness of expression.

The Prime Minister is also likely to know whether your advice is worth taking since, while not eavesdropping on your every action, he will be kept reasonably well informed of the quality of your contribution to the government's work. His sources will be his Private Office, operating on the Private Office net, the Secretary of the Cabinet, communicating regularly with Permanent Secretaries, study of your contributions to Cabinet Committees of which he is chairman, and careful perusal of the Hansard reports of Parliamentary proceedings. James Callaghan, in particular, was as Prime Minister a devoted student of Hansard and would also occasionally drop into Question Time to see how his ministerial colleagues were getting on. He would not hesitate, sitting on the front bench, to give them a ticking off if need be, as I once heard him do to a junior minister who, permitted somewhat unusually to attend a meeting of the National Economic Development Council, had taken advantage of his opportunity to disagree publicly with the views expressed at the meeting by a senior Cabinet minister.

The Prime Minister may even, possibly in public, bestow praise upon you. It will be nice if it happens. Do not count on it, though. But the Prime Minister is not there as a version of some male (or female) headmistress of a girls' school, whose favour is to be curried and approval cause gratified simpers. He is there to be used: used sparingly, as an ultimate deterrent. For even the threat of intervention from Number Ten can obtain action where before there was inertia. And an actual intervention can really get things moving. It is, however, vital to choose your issue accurately. Get it wrong, and you will lose any ground you have so far gained. Get it right, and you can achieve complete success. The key is to select an area of policy in which the Prime Minister is interested to begin with.

Take shipbuilding, for example. Imagine that you are involved in negotiations to secure a massive order from a foreign country, an order so huge that the work it will provide can prevent the closure of several shipyards in areas of high unemployment. Take into account that shipbuilding orders are so hard to come by that complicated and possibly even unprecedented financing techniques are necessary to secure them. Imagine that you, with the aid of talented officials, have worked out such techniques but that their novelty – though their probity is unquestioned, and will afterwards publicly be seen to be so in a report by a Parliamentary Select Committee – is arousing resistance in certain traditionalist quarters in Whitehall. Imagine, in fact, that you are stuck.

In this situation recall that the Prime Minister has shown a particular concern for shipbuilding policy. Accordingly, take a deep breath and send the Prime Minister a minute telling him that, much as you would like the deal to go through, it looks as if it may not be possible. Then sit back and wait. If you are lucky a response will come from the Number Ten Private Office ('The Prime Minister has seen your Minister's minute . . .') instructing that a special meeting be held to consider the problem. It may even request that Harold Lever, Chancellor of the Duchy of Lancaster, roving hitman of the Cabinet, and the ultimate deterrent's ultimate deterrent, be involved. The meeting takes place. Techniques even more ingenious than those originally contemplated are approved. After the kind of tough last-minute negotiations for which the customer country is noted the deal is triumphantly concluded, many thousands of jobs are saved, and the Opposition have hell knocked out of them when they attempt to censure you in the House of Commons. That is one example of how the weight of the office of Prime Minister can be brought into play by a minister lucky enough to hit upon exactly the right issue.

The converse, of course, is that the Prime Minister may also intervene when you do not want him to. He may feel that your handling of a problem, though impeccable in theory, is not going to get the result that he needs politically. He may even, this time against your will and to your annoyance, inject Harold Lever into the situation. If he does, do not get cross. Remember that he is looking after the interests of the whole government while you, like all your colleagues, are subject to fits of departmentalitis, a disease to which he is constitutionally immune. Sit back and enjoy it.

Harold Wilson once said that he wanted to make Number Ten the powerhouse of Whitehall. I am not sure he was right, and that that is the proper role for a tiny office of a few people trying to cope with many large departments involved in a never-ceasing mass of almost intractable problems. You may, however, find that Number Ten is a very effective weedkiller in the Whitehall garden. And that could suit you very well, because there will be many weeds for you to kill.

9

How to Operate in Parliament

Though your officials would be perfectly happy for you to remain permanently in your department and totally in their thrall, fortunately for you (and in fact for them) you will have many duties to perform in the House of Commons. Indeed your department will have a parliamentary branch especially established to facilitate your dealings with both Houses.

Sitting on the government front bench for the first time is an experience you will always remember. Speaking from the Dispatch Box for the first time is equally memorable, but as an ordeal.

It is a toss-up whether that first Dispatch Box appearance will be at Question Time or in an adjournment debate. In my case it was an adjournment, which was a gentle initiation. The proceedings of the House of Commons consist of making decisions on Questions. These, to be confusing, are not the questions that you answer – or evade answering – at Question Time. If a Bill has a Second Reading the Speaker informs the House: 'The Question is the Bill be now read a Second Time.' The House cannot even adjourn for the day without being called upon to agree to the proposition: 'The Question is this House do now adjourn.' The custom has grown up that when this Question is put at the end of the day's business there should be a short debate upon it. Just to be even more confusing, there can be other debates at other times on a Question that the House adjourn. These are generally debates initiated in prime debating time by the government or the Opposition. At the end of the debate the motion is either withdrawn or defeated by the government's majority, the House then going on to other items of business. Sometimes, when the Labour government had no majority, this kind of motion to adjourn was carried against the government's wishes but it still had the effect of adjourning the House. Everyone went home early wishing (except for the Government Chief Whip, of course) that the government could be defeated more often.

My adjournment debate was not on one of these highly charged occasions but a quiet discussion initiated by a back-bencher. If you are a back-bencher and you wish to raise in the House of Commons the problem of a hospital in your constituency or – much more likely these days, I fear – the sudden deportation of a Pakistani constituent, you will write in to the Speaker saying you would like to raise the matter on the adjournment. A ballot is held on Thursday to decide to which MPs the end-of-business adjournment debates will be allocated for the following week, with the Speaker having the additional right to select one back-bencher from the list of applicants. This ensures that if you have been unlucky in the ballot several weeks running you will in the end get your debate either late at night on the adjournment or in one of the Wednesday morning sittings initiated by the renowned (or, according to taste, reviled) Jopling reforms. The Speaker's Secretary (a great power, who stands next to the Speaker at Question Time and during ministerial statements, nudging her as to which member should catch her eye) will write to you telling you whether you have won or lost. He can slightly overdo this, and once wrote to tell me that I had lost when I had not even applied.

The list of winners is also posted in the No Division Lobby, which is a kind of notice board for MPs, containing also the programme of business for next week, lists of amendments selected by the Speaker for debate in Report Stage proceedings, and details of which MPs will be getting an allocation of tickets for the public gallery (so that you can nag them to give them up to you for a visiting school party). Junior ministers go along every Thursday to look at the notice board and see whether they have drawn the short straw of replying to an adjournment debate the following week. Brynmor John, when he was Minister of State at the Home Office, at one time found himself replying to so many adjournment debates that colleagues suggested that he had won the adjournment half-hour outright.

Your adjournment debate, then, comes on at the end of all other business, early in the afternoon on Fridays but generally no earlier than 10 p.m. and sometimes very much later on other days. You, as the minister scheduled to reply, absolutely have to be there; if you are not, there is a tremendous row. In my case the debate came reasonably early and the Conservative Member (Kenneth Clarke, who later became a junior minister with adjournment debates of his own to answer and later still a Cabinet minister, spared from having to go anywhere near adjournment debates) had chosen the subject of mobile homes: caravans, in fact. My department, as soon as it found out about the debate, had immediately prepared a speech for me. Preparing a speech for a minister is all part of the presumption by the department that, unless proved otherwise, their minister is an imbecile. If they prepare a speech for him it will certainly be full of thuses, hences and hithertos, but it will make some kind of sense, will not contravene stated government policy and, even if the minister is too inarticulate to read it out intelligibly, can be taken up to the Hansard office by his Private Secretary and will look quite respectable when it appears in print.

I, though, was a new broom, and was having none of that; I would write my own speech. Afterwards I learned quite quickly that with adjournment debates there was little point in this. It was not as though the House would be full of turbulent throngs to be thrilled or appalled by my oratory; the only people present would be the weary Deputy Speaker occupying the chair, the MP, raising the debate, myself as minister, and a government Whip there to ensure that I did not make a mess of getting the House properly adjourned. In my five years in the government I persisted in writing all my own speeches for major debates, but for adjournment debates and other routine or technical occasions I would tell the department roughly what I would like them to put in a draft which, when it arrived, I would rewrite to suit my own speaking habits.

On this first occasion, though, I was on my mettle. I had meetings with officials – who must wearily have resigned themselves to all this fuss about a simple adjournment debate – decided on the line I would take, and got down to composing my polished text. I should point out that it is very easy to write an adjournment speech, since the debate almost always lasts exactly half an hour, with the back-bench MP speaking for the first fifteen minutes or so, and the minister filling the rest of the time; so you do not actually have to prepare yourself for the cut and thrust of debate. For my speech I wanted to quote a poem about caravans which I vaguely remem-bered from my schooldays, but could not track it down. My lovely

Angela, who had come into the civil service straight from teaching at an infants' school, made enquiries at her old school, all to no avail. So I had to do without the poem. But the children at the school all wrote me poems about caravans that they made up themselves, illustrated by pictures they drew. These were so charming that I had them framed and put up on my office wall.

You will find that the actual debate passes off peaceably enough, and you then get into your government car and go off home to do your red box. You are lucky that you will no longer be a victim of the Consolidated Fund Bill, an ordeal by oratory swept away by the Jopling reforms. On the Consolidated Fund Bill, MPs were allowed to discuss almost anything at all. So the Bill was turned into a back-benchers' occasion, and MPs entered a ballot, with the subjects they wanted to raise being allotted numbers. Once again the junior ministers were given the job of replying, and when the ballot was declared they clustered around the No Lobby notice board to see whether they had been unlucky enough to be caught.

You were all right if you were the minister due to reply to debate Number One. That came at a civilized hour. But if you got debate Number Thirteen, for example, you were likely to be required in the early hours of the morning. Your Private Secretary usually made an arrangement with the policeman behind the Speaker's chair – who knows absolutely everything – to telephone when, say, debate Number Ten was reached. The Private Secretary then telephoned your driver who, happily on overtime, whisked round to your home to take you to the House to reply to the debate. The form generally resembled that of adjournment debates (unless a group of Labour members raised London housing, a traditional fiendish exercise in sadism which, happily, they refrained from carrying out against one of their own ministers) except for the ungodliness of the hour. There was, however, a snag. You might have two debates to reply to, Numbers Seven and Thirteen. It simply was not worth going home between the two, so you just had to settle down in your room for an all-night vigil.

Sometimes, if a particular debate looked like taking place at an impossible hour, you would be able to come to an arrangement with the back-bench MP who had won that number in the ballot. He would agree to withdraw his debate in return, say, for a helpful letter from you which he could publish in his local newspaper.

You could both then go home to bed like civilized human beings. Sometimes an MP would withdraw his debate without telling you, leaving you to hang around until you discovered that you were doing so to no purpose. Happily, few MPs would do this to their most hated opponent. On one occasion, though, arriving bright and early for a Consolidated Fund Bill debate I was due to answer at about 8 a.m., I went into the Tea Room for a cup of coffee and found Shirley Summerskill, then the waspishly witty MP for Halifax and a junior minister at the Home Office, sitting there looking decidedly wan. It turned out that she had had one debate at around 2 a.m. and had then waited to answer another which was due to come on roughly at 6 a.m. But the MP concerned, a member of her own party and known to everyone as the most swinish of all Labour MPs, had withdrawn the debate without notifying the minister.

Question Time is a much more lively occasion, the first substantial business every day from Monday to Thursday, with the House always reasonably crowded. Each department comes up first on the list for answering questions every three, four or five weeks or so. Questions can be tabled as early as two weeks before they are due to be answered orally, and generally on the first day a batch will be tabled sufficient in number for the department to get to work on the replies. The question printed on the Order Paper is generally innocuous: 'To ask the Secretary of State for Industry' – all questions have to be addressed to the Secretary of State, whichever minister actually answers them – 'when he last met the Chairman of British Aerospace.' The trick, of course, is to try to anticipate what the Member will ask in the supplementary question he is entitled to put. If it is a member of your own party he will probably be asking something that will get him a helpful report in his local newspaper; if a member of the Opposition, he will want to ambush you with some catch question. So you are provided with a loose-leaf folder which contains the main answer, further pages suggesting answers to possible supplementary questions, and background notes as well. These notes will attempt, to no great avail, to rummage around in the questioner's psychology and try to sort out why on earth he put down his question.

Well before the day for your Question Time approaches, Parliamentary branch will circulate among ministers a suggested allocation of questions between all of you, to ensure that you each get a fair ration. This can be queried, the final decision being that of the Secretary of State. Some ministers are particularly anxious to answer certain questions – or questioners – some just as anxious to dodge them. You will be sent up in draft the answers to the questions you have been allocated, and will change the answers if you do not think them suitable. You will then, if you have any sense, search your political memory for weak points in the parliamentary record of any troublesome Opposition member and prepare to floor him if you can manage it. When the Department of Industry (i.e., in this case, myself) was having to consider whether to renew the licence which allowed the Hull City Council, alone in the country, to run its own telephone service independently of the Post Office (more about *that* later) a Conservative Member of Parliament, Michael Neubert, put down a question about it. I recollected hazily in my mind that he had once voted against a Private Member's Bill put forward by a Labour MP which aimed at extending the powers of local councils to run commercial services. The Department of the Environment confirmed this from its records, so that when Neubert asked his expected supplementary question championing the renewal of Hull's licence I was able to remind him of his earlier misdeed and welcome his conversion to municipal socialism. That got no one anywhere, but was at any rate good clean fun and went down well with Hull's Labour MPs.

The temptation is, indeed, to resort almost solely to flippancy in your replies, since as minister you have the last word and it boosts your ego to get an easy laugh. I was clearly overdoing this when at the Department of the Environment and one evening Anthony Crosland, the Secretary of State, invited me to dinner at his home. While his wife was out of the room he offered me a drink and, with his back turned while he poured from the decanter, he said to me: 'Gerald, you have arrived at a stage in your career when you must try to be less *frivolous*.' This was his severest word of condemnation, and it was extremely kind of him to take so much trouble over me. I reformed – at any rate for a time. In fact, I did my best and you should too to abide by Harold Wilson's sage rule: answer a question in the spirit in which it is asked. I only occasionally departed from this and when I did, slapping down serious questions from Tory MPs like David Price and Peter Emery, I felt ashamed.

But oral questions are not the only ones you will have to answer. Dozens of questions come in every day for which written replies are sought, and junior ministers generally answer almost all of these. There are formulae for answering some of these, referring Members to cited publications rather than giving them the substantive information they request. You may think, as I did, that it is unfair on MPs, particularly those of your own party, to fob them off in this way; but you will find your department very hard to convince, since to change a standard formula sets a precedent; and precedents are the Bible of the civil service. On one occasion I insisted, against great resistance, that a Labour MP be given the information he wanted rather than simply be fobbed off with the name of a reference book. People of ever-increasing rank kept coming to see me, seeking to change my mind. They spent far more time on this than would have been taken in answering the question. When the most senior supplicant of all pleaded that the precedents were all against me, I retorted that I was now and hereby setting a new precedent. The great strength of the civil service is their readiness to wear you down in what they regard as a good cause; they reckon – and often they are right – that they can simply tire you into submission.

All of these events are, however, child's play compared with the major parliamentary occasions. When your department is involved in a set-piece debate lasting all day with a division at 10 p.m. the Secretary of State generally speaks first, in mid-afternoon, while the minister next in rank winds up, speaking generally from 9.30 to 10 p.m. If you get this assignment you will find it one of the most exciting occasions in your parliamentary life. Especially towards the end of your speech, as MPs crowd into the Chamber and stand at the Bar of the House ready for the Division, you may have a near-capacity audience. If the subject is contentious, the atmosphere will be very rowdy; you may have trouble making yourself heard; once I gave way to an MP who intervened simply because I had lost my voice. But if you are able to rise to the occasion you will enjoy a heady parliamentary triumph that will have you walking several feet above the ground.

There are techniques you can try to learn for such an occasion, just as there are for any testing job. Your very physical location will help you, since it is much easier speaking from the Dispatch Box (placed on the table between the two front benches) than from a back bench. This is because your notes are in front of you resting on the Dispatch Box, and you do not have the problem of what you do with your hands, as you do on the back benches. Do not waste your good lines – if you have any – at the start of your speech, because MPs will at that stage still be drifting into the Chamber. Try to get some laughs early on; they will put your supporters in a good mood. Try to goad some of the more vulnerable Opposition MPs into intervening in your speech, and have ready a weakness in their political (never personal) record with which to respond to their intervention. You can make sure they will be present by sending them notes – an expected courtesy in any case – telling them that you intend to refer to them. They will be too curious not to turn up, and too furious not to intervene. Then you will have them. The files of the Department of Industry, for example, were always bulging with letters from Conservative MPs pleading for government expenditure on projects in their constituencies; to quote these against them in a debate in which the Opposition was censuring the Labour government for excessive expenditure was guaranteed to cause acute discomfiture. Yet even so the letters kept on coming in.

Always give way to interventions early on in your speech. This will enable you to refuse to do so later on and give you, with luck, a long uninterrupted stretch in which you can develop your case or extend your diatribe, whichever course you have decided to follow. If possible plan the pace of your speech. At a given moment, which you should calculate to the very word, it will if you are lucky take off and almost start to fly. If this works as you have planned, it can be a wonderful feeling. Always prepare less material than will fill the time allotted to you, since interruptions in the middle of your speech, additions to your prepared remarks to take account of points made in the debate, and uproar at the end will certainly take up some of your precious minutes.

Your final paragraphs should be grandiloquent even if almost meaningless. Little of them will in any case be heard in the uproar, but you need a sentence on which you can sit down to a cheer. And make sure you get your cheer. If the debate is on an Opposition motion, the other party's Chief Whip will attempt to end the debate by moving the closure to the debate before you have finished speaking, thus forcing you to subside into your seat in anti-climax. The trick is to watch the digital clock hanging from the gallery

opposite you and finish speaking a few seconds after it has signalled
9.59 p.m. Your back-benchers will then cheer you safely through to
the vote at 10 o'clock. All this sounds like theatre, and in a way it is.
The House of Commons is, after all, a debating chamber. In any
case, your back-benchers like to be cheered up. Of course there will
be other more subdued occasions, when it will be out of place for
you to make an aggressive rhetorical foray. A quieter conver-
sational tone will be needed and that should be cultivated too.

Your speech may be on a motion for debate – the steel industry,
the Polish shipbuilding order – or it may be on the Second Reading
of a Bill. If it is a Bill, the Second Reading will be followed by
Committee Stage. Do not be deluded into believing that, having
scored a triumph in the Second Reading by knocking the Opposition about, you should the following week walk into the
Committee Room on the floor above the Chamber in the same
aggressive mood. Your aim in the debate on the floor of the House
was to win a political debating victory. Your objective in the Committee is to secure the passage of your Bill with the least possible
delay. In the Chamber you were buttressed by a majority of votes,
however exiguous. The Committee is much smaller in size, a cross-
section of the House possibly numbering two dozen or fewer. In the
Committee you may still have a majority, but the Opposition will
have the whip hand.

In a debate on Second Reading, or any other major debate on the
floor of the House, Opposition members can speak only once and
the time for the whole debate is strictly limited. In Committee they
can speak as many times as they like and as long as they like,
provided they remain within the rules of order, which in Committee
are pretty lax anyhow. Any aggressive speech by you will only
provoke them to be aggressive back, and at great length. A long
speech by you will challenge them to be even longer. An intervention by you in one of their speeches will provoke them into
replying to your intervention, at very great length.

So you need to alter your behaviour – indeed, alter your parliamentary personality – completely. You should seek to pacify, not to
provoke. You should speak briefly. You should keep the spokesmen
on the Opposition side, including the representatives of the minor
parties, informed of every move you mean to make – excepting
those you need to reserve to yourself. You should provide every

item of information that Committee members request, in writing if you cannot supply it at the sitting; if need be, you should inundate the Committee with informative correspondence. You should compliment Opposition speakers on the constructive way in which they have moved their amendments even if you cannot actually accept their amendments. You should refrain from questioning the technical adequacy of the amendments, even when they are technically inadequate. Where you can accept amendments, you should. Oppositions will in the nature of things table amendments to Bills which, however contentious the legislation, are either actually constructive or at any rate meaningless enough to be incorporated into the eventual Act without actually damaging it. Your department will on the whole be against your accepting any amendments. But it is for you, as the politician, to gauge the temperature of the Committee and decide when, without interfering of course with the substance of the Bill, it is best to make a concession.

Sometimes, in any case, you will have to. Although your great aim as a minister is to achieve absolute silence among your own back-bench members in order to help speed the measure on its way, some of the government members on the Committee may be sufficiently and inconveniently interested in the legislation to want to improve it from their own point of view. Unless dissuaded they will move amendments. And sometimes the Opposition will be mischievous enough to support the amendments just for the pleasure of bringing about a government defeat. Always accept your own back-benchers' amendments if you can – and do so immediately after they have been moved, to cut down the length of debate. If you cannot accept the substance, give them an assurance that you will consider their point and try to come forward with a suitable amendment of your own on Report Stage, the next stage in the consideration of the Bill when it returns to the floor of the House.

Occasionally your party colleagues will persist, and the Opposition will help them to defeat you. This happened on the Committee Stage of the 1975 Industry Bill, when the Conservatives joined with some Labour MPs to write into the Bill an obligation on the Treasury to publish periodic economic forecasts. Time, though, brings in his revenges, and it was as a result of this provision that the new Conservative government was compelled at the end of 1979 to publish a horrendous economic forecast for 1980.

Your wiles on the Committee may not succeed, and the Opposition may start to spin out the proceedings. You will then move a Sittings Motion, increasing the number of days and hours on which the Committee will sit. The Opposition will then table more amendments than ever, and make longer speeches about them. In the end you will need a Guillotine Motion to bring the proceedings to an end. This on the whole is always likely to happen, at some stage, on an extremely contentious Bill, such as the measure to nationalize the aircraft and shipbuilding industries which I piloted through the Commons, and whose Committee Stage was enshrined in the *Guinness Book of Records* as having had the greatest number of sittings in the history of Parliament.

On a less contentious Bill, though, a forthcoming and amenable approach by the minister in charge really can save time. By accepting an Opposition amendment that merely put into the Bill what the government intended to do anyhow, I managed to get the whole Committee consideration of a Post Office Bill over in less than a single 150-minute sitting. I secured the speedy passage of the Shipbuilding Redundancy Payments Bill by another device. Governments do have other resources at their command besides guillotines and winning ways. The most effective is the Money Resolution.

Every Bill that involves expenditure has to be accompanied by a Money Resolution authorizing that expenditure, which the House passes immediately after agreeing to the Bill's Second Reading. No amendment to the Bill can be debated, let alone voted upon, if it is outside the scope of the Money Resolution. So you will take great care to limit the scope for amendment not only by making your Bill as short as possible but by having your Money Resolution drawn as tight as possible. You will recall that in Chapter 6 I described how we decided to exclude private shiprepair concerns from the government's redundancy payments scheme. When the enabling Bill came before its Standing Committee the Opposition sought to move amendments that would include the private yards. They were unable to do so; the Money Resolution excluded them. A constitutional oddity then followed.

The House of Lords is not bound by the Commons rules of order

– or indeed by any rules of order whatever. Conservative peers therefore voted, when the Bill reached the Lords, in favour of amendments to include the private yards and demanded that, when the Bill returned to the Commons, the government – who alone have the power to move Money Resolutions – should put forward the necessary Resolution to make their amendments valid. I refused to do any such thing, and was strongly supported by the Prime Minister. When the Bill accordingly reappeared before the Commons, the Speaker solemnly announced that the Lords amendments were an assault upon the privileges of the Commons, ruled that the amendments could not even be discussed, and instructed the House to reject them forthwith. This the House meekly (and in the government's case delightedly) did, and the Bill passed into law in the form desired by the Commons and the government.

Treat the House cursorily or insultingly, and it will punish you. I had to eat humble pie when, on a Housing Bill, I accused the Opposition of taking a different attitude to a clause on Report Stage compared to the stand they had adopted on it in Committee. In fact the clause had been re-numbered between Committee and Report, and the Opposition had been absolutely consistent in their approach. Treat the House with courtesy and take it seriously, recognize that Members of Parliament speak not only for themselves but for the many thousands they represent, and you will earn respect even from those who disagree most strongly with you. Beware over-confidence; for my part I have never once, from the front bench or the back benches, in government or Opposition, at major events or on trivial occasions, risen to address the House without feelings of intense nervousness. If you think administration is the be-all and end-all of ministerial life, and regard the Commons as an irritating distraction that has somehow to be coped with, the Commons will make you miserable when they have it in their power to do so. If you regard Parliament as your highest priority, and take the trouble to let it know that you do, you will experience in it the most fulfilling moments in your ministerial life.

10

How to Work with Your Parliamentary Colleagues

When a new government is being formed, the members of the majority party will be afflicted by a wave of nervousness. Will they get a job? It is legendary (but true all the same) that MPs fear to stray far from their telephones in case they miss the fateful call. One Labour MP, who before entering Parliament used to act as election agent for the veteran Member he eventually succeeded, told me that after it was clear by the day after polling that Labour had won the 1964 election, the candidate whose successful campaign he had managed refused to leave the local election headquarters to undertake his traditional post-polling-day tour of the constituency, so confident was he that at any moment a message would come through from Downing Street offering him the Cabinet post he was sure he would get and was even more sure he deserved. As the day went on and no call came, he grew increasingly morose; and after that he was always a bitter man.

Following a general election the allocation of the more junior ministerial posts may still be taking place by the time that Parliament has reassembled for the swearing-in of Members. MPs will sit round the Tea Room, exchanging nervous jokes or unconvincingly pretending not to be interested. From time to time a colleague will turn to you and ask, in as casual a manner as he can assume: 'Have you heard from Number Ten yet?' If your answer is no, he will subside with relief. If you have not heard either, then there is still a chance for him; or at any rate he is not alone in having been passed over. In the end, however, you will have received a call and very many of your colleagues will not.

Do not expect them to be pleased. When they find out that you have been appointed while they have not, many will take the trouble to congratulate you and most of these will be sincere. Some, however, very ostentatiously will not. When I was promoted to be a Minister of State, in a minor reshuffle at the end of 1975, I happened to be sitting in the Tea Room with a friend, who was an Under-Secretary of State, when the news came through on the news agency tape machine which is situated outside the Smoking Room. Many Members who saw it were generous enough to stop at my table as they passed by and offer me their good wishes; the friend I was sitting with, his brow black as thunder, said nothing.

However, even those who sincerely congratulate you will not be undilutedly delighted. Some of them will have sat in Parliament longer than you, and will feel they have merited office more than you. Even your contemporaries and juniors will feel – very likely rightly – that given the chance they could do the job as well as you, if not better. It is up to you to convince them that you are at least making the most, in the interests of the government and the party, of your good fortune in receiving an opportunity which they have been denied. So do your very best to be good at your job. I once overheard an outspoken back-bencher tell a junior minister somewhat brutally: 'Nobody likes you, but what exasperates and amazes them is that you are showing ability.' If you cannot be liked, be respected.

Remember that you are not only a member of the government, but a Member of Parliament elected by the same electoral processes as your colleagues. Do not assume airs of superiority just because you got a call from Number Ten and they did not. Above all, do not vanish from their company. Some MPs, upon being appointed to government, disappear from Parliament as if swallowed up in a huge pit. One Conservative MP, appointed a Minister of State in 1979, complained to me on one of his rare appearances in the Palace of Westminster that his duties kept him away from the Palace. They did not; he simply preferred it that way.

Refuse all those invitations to trade association lunches and dinners, where you will eat expensive processed food in the company of political opponents before delivering a speech which will never be reported, and instead eat cheap processed food in the House of Commons Tea Room, Cafeteria or Members' Dining Room in the company of your own colleagues. One fellow minister in the Labour government once said to me, as we were riding together in a government car on the way to the House of

Commons, 'Don't you find it terrible having to go to all these lunches?' He genuinely did not realize that he did not have to do any such thing. One senior minister, it is true, accepted every lunch and dinner to which he was invited because he was rather parsimonious and liked eating free; on the rare occasions when invitations were not forthcoming he ate a heavily subsidized meal in his department's canteen, and thus gained a reputation among officials for being democratic. His parliamentary colleagues, though, never saw him and when he decided to leave politics did not notice that he had gone.

The House of Commons Tea Room, in particular, is the place where MPs while away odd periods they have to fill in between debates, committees and other engagements. It is by convention a semi-segregated room with the front half, leading off the Ways and Means Corridor, customarily being occupied by Labour MPs, while a rear section, though containing a table claimed by Welsh Labour MPs and an area mainly used by Scottish MPs, is the reserve of Conservatives, who need less space because they on the whole prefer the Smoking Room. Harold Wilson, James Callaghan and Margaret Thatcher, as Prime Ministers, were all noted for mingling with their back-benchers as regular patrons of the Tea Room, though few could recall Edward Heath ever having set foot in it. The most cynical condemnation possible of a Labour front-bencher is that his appearance in the Tea Room is the signal for the muttered comment: 'There must be an election coming' (the Parliamentary Labour Party being prone to electing Members from among its ranks for various purposes, and sudden unaccustomed appearance in the Tea Room being regarded as a form of canvassing). Be sufficient of a regular in the Tea Room to make this comment out of place in your case. Who knows? You may enjoy it.

Remember that as a minister you have privileges denied to your back-bench colleagues. One of the most prized (as you will find when you lose it) is your official car. This is particularly useful when the House finishes its business late at night, taxis at that time being hard to come by and very expensive in any case. Nothing is more maddening for back-bench MPs waiting in vain at the taxi stand outside the Members' Cloakroom at 2 a.m. for a cab to come and pick them up than to see you sweeping by, the sole passenger in the ministerial car that has been solicitously waiting for you beyond the archway in Speaker's Court. After all, the back-benchers have been kept behind at the House to cast a vote that sustains the government in office and keeps you in your ministerial job and car. Have the grace to stop your car and offer a lift to anyone going your way.

Remember, too, that you have access to information and can have recourse to actions that can be of great assistance to back-bench colleagues. Bear in mind that the least rewarding role in Parliament is that of a government back-bencher, who does not even have the outlet of being able to attack the government (consistently at any rate) but is simply expected to vote obediently in support of it. You may derisively be referred to as part of the payroll vote; and while it is true that you are required to vote for the government perpetually whatever your views on individual policies may be, you are indeed being paid extra for it. Your colleagues have to do it out of sheer loyalty, and be referred to for their pains even more disrespectfully as Lobby fodder.

So bear in mind that your colleagues have to go back to their constituencies and defend the government if they can and, even if they cannot or do not wish to defend the government, they will still be blamed for its shortcomings and, still worse, lose votes. You have an obligation to them. They will accost you in the Tea Room (if you go there) or the Division Lobby (where you have to go) with requests for information that affects their constituencies. Always make a point of helping. Give them the number of your Private Office line at the department so that they do not have to wait, fuming, for a response from the clogged departmental switchboard. If they ask you for material relating to their constituencies, take some trouble over composing a letter that they can have published in their local newspaper.

If they have tabled a parliamentary question to you, written or oral, remember that they have done so because they want something out of it; make sure they get it. If need be, ask them what answer they want and, if at all possible, provide it. When they raise a subject on the adjournment, again ask them what kind of reply will suit them best. From time to time they will ask you to receive delegations of their constituents (more about these in Chapter 14). Even if you have nothing positive you can offer, always agree. You may have no idea of how helpful it can be to an MP simply to shepherd his constituents into an imposing ministerial office in the general region of Whitehall. Similarly, if they ask you to visit their constituency for a tour of factories or housing estates, or to address a political meeting, always go, even though they may not afterwards be blatantly grateful. I visited the marginal constituency of one MP three times, and was afterwards blasted by him at a meeting of the Parliamentary Labour Party for being insufficiently responsive to party feeling. I felt pretty bruised at the time, but afterwards consoled myself by imagining the abuse he would have poured on me if I had refused to go, or indeed gone only twice. He did hold his very marginal seat in the subsequent election by 621 votes, and maybe I was responsible for the 21.

You will have decisions to make in your department relating to the constituencies of your back-bench colleagues. Do your best, within the rules of propriety, to tilt those decisions in their favour. It can help a lot. In the October 1974 election I toured derelict housing estates in a colleague's marginal constituency, and was much impressed by the poor conditions and the need for rehabilitation, which was forcibly impressed upon me not only by the MP but by a local La Pasionaria of the estate tenants' association. Returning to my department after the election, I found that while I could not make money available directly for the necessary modernization, I could allocate additional funds to the council which they could then use to make the estate less horrible. I did so and, though the appalling Tory council concerned pocketed the cash without using it on that estate, I still get Christmas cards from La Pasionaria.

Be imaginative enough to realize that the kind of briefing which, after you have been at your department for only a few weeks, you already take for granted, is not available to your back-bench colleagues. If, for your various purposes, you want to know how many men it would take to crew sixteen bulk carriers, or at what date the Conservative Party began publishing its annual accounts, your department will have ways of finding out for you. The Private Office net will ensure, also, that you can get information you require relating to the work of other departments. The back-bench MP has to rely on his research assistant, if his Parliamentary allowance allows him to run to having one, or on the excellent but greatly overstretched facilities of the House of Commons Library. So provide him yourself with material for his speeches; after all, these will often be in support of the government. Provide him, too, with briefs on your department's actions which you, of course, know backwards but with which he cannot be expected to be conversant. Invite him to your department and give him access to civil servants who specialize in subjects that concern him. Arrange meetings at your department for groups of interested back-benchers.

After all, you are all members of the same Parliamentary Labour Party. So make sure that you attend the regular meetings of the full party and keep abreast of what is going on; this is an effective remedy against the onset of departmentalitis. You will in any case be expected to be at the Thursday-evening Party Meeting that considers next week's business, ready to answer questions about any legislation relating to your own department. There are other meetings you can attend too. These do not include the back-bench groups which consider specific policy areas – if you turn up at one of these it will gently be indicated to you that such occasions are not for you – but very much do include the regional groups. Your party will have groups specially set up to consider matters relating to geographical areas such as the West Midlands and the North West. All the MPs for a region are automatically members of such groups, whether ministers or not, so you can attend your group meetings, taking part in the routine business but also providing information about government actions affecting the region. A lady from the Levenshulme ward in my own constituency once wrote to me, reprimanding me for what she felt to be the government's neglect of the North-West area. I therefore accumulated information relating to the government's record which, when put together in one document, was really very impressive. I not only sent the document to my constituent but distributed it to the members of the North-West Group of Labour MPs, regularly updating it. It became known as the Lady from Levenshulme brief and I believe was found useful.

Your colleagues should not only be informed, they should be consulted. During the currency of the Lib-Lab pact the Cabinet rightly felt that if the Liberals had to be consulted about everything that the government did, then the Parliamentary Labour Party must be consulted as well. So it became the practice to consult the subject groups about all pending legislation; many ministers had, in any case, done this long before the Lib-Lab pact, getting themselves invited to the groups related to their own departments, discussing their problems and seeking advice.

Take special care to do this when one of your department's Bills is going through its Committee Stage. You should hold regular weekly meetings with your party's members on the Standing Committee, to keep them informed of the government's attitude (otherwise, they may think you are yielding important policy points to the Opposition on which, in fact, you have every intention of standing firm) and discuss tactics with them. This can be very important when the government is hard pressed while seeking the passage of contentious legislation.

During the very short Parliament of March–September 1974, Reginald Freeson and I were given the task of steering through Parliament the Rent Bill, designed to give security of tenure to tenants of privately let furnished premises. Everyone knew that an election would be coming in the autumn, and the aim of the Conservatives was to delay this legislation in the hope that they could win the election and kill it. Labour MPs, on the other hand, were desperate that it should be passed, fearing that if it was not hundreds of thousands of unprotected tenants would face eviction. The Labour members of the Standing Committee met and agreed that, whatever the difficulties they would have to undergo, everything must be done to get the Bill on to the Statute Book.

The Conservatives, who had not dared to vote against the Bill on Second Reading, decided to obstruct it in Committee, with the intention of preventing the conclusion of the Committee Stage before the summer recess and the expected dissolution of Parliament. They started in earnest one Thursday morning and we for our part decided that we would simply go on sitting until the Committee Stage was concluded or nearly so. The Committee sat, including meal breaks, for twenty-seven hours. National attention was focused on this marathon, since ministers and Members kept walking out of the Committee Room to give radio interviews about it; the Conservatives' nerve broke, and we got our legislation through. This would not have been possible if our back-benchers had not agreed to carry the burden.

You will find that a government retreat, just as much as a government achievement, is made easier by proper consultation. The troubled passage through Parliament of the Bill to nationalize the aircraft and shipbuilding industries reached the nadir of its fortunes when Examiners ruled that the section on shiprepair was technically faulty; the government, by now without a majority, was faced with the dilemma of either abandoning the nationalization of shiprepair or risking the loss of the whole Bill. Very reluctantly, since I had been an ardent advocate of including shiprepair, I recommended that it be removed from the Bill; I suggested, however, that since the Parliamentary Labour Party had taken particular trouble to support this section, with many sick MPs coming to the House especially to vote on it, we should conduct consultations with our back-benchers before dropping it. The Prime Minister very cogently asked what we would do if the consultations turned out adverse to my recommendation; a question to which I had no reply. Fortunately, however, the Labour Members of the Standing Committee, called together to discuss the matter, agreed with only one dissentient with the government's proposal; we were able to move the necessary amendments without the embarrassment of any of our back-bench colleagues voting against us.

Remember, however, that though you as the minister will collect any kudos for the passage of a popular though contentious Bill, it will have been the back-benchers, and particularly those on the Standing Committee, who by their votes and attendance were actually responsible for the achievement. So it will do no harm to thank them publicly. It will do no harm either to hold a celebratory party and invite them to it.

As a minister you will be called upon to be host at other receptions too. When you cannot get out of carrying out this awful chore, which involves standing at the entrance to the reception hall with a fixed leer on your face while you shake hands with hundreds of guests until your arm feels as if it will fall off, do at least make sure that a reasonable number of your back-bench colleagues are invited. If at all possible, invite their wives or husbands too, since they have an even worse time of it than their spouses.

When you reply to a debate, do not just look for oratorical laurels for yourself, but be sure to refer to the speeches of as many of your colleagues as possible; they like to feel that they have not spoken for nothing. If you can, pay tribute to them for the pressure they have put on you to bring about the popular decision you have just announced. In short, as my parents would have put it, remember that each of them too is a mother's child.

If you do all of this, and more, do not delude yourself that your colleagues will actually be reconciled to your having been preferred over them; but they may at any rate tolerate your holding the job they could not have. And, if your party loses the following election, you may hope to be welcomed back among them with reasonable cordiality. You may even be able to walk into the Tea Room without provoking cynical remarks behind the buttered scones.

11

How to Keep in Touch with Your Party

Way out there beyond Whitehall and Westminster, is your party – the political party which you joined, probably many years ago, and whose name appears beside yours on the ballot paper to identify you to those few voters in your constituency who are not fully acquainted with your formidable record. You know that it is the traditional and faithful support for your party by thousands of voters that has secured your own election to Parliament. You know, too, that it is your duty as a Member of Parliament, and your even greater duty as a minister, to bring about fulfilment of your party's principles to the greatest extent that you can. You should bear in mind that the eminence, such as it is, that you have achieved as a minister and MP has been won for you over decades by selfless people whose toil and drudgery have kept the party going during its worst times. You will know people like this personally in your constituency, and you will meet them as you travel round the country. You owe them your best efforts in return for theirs.

Your party is spread over more than six hundred constituencies all over Great Britain. Your most regular contact with it, outside your own constituency, will be with your party headquarters. There at Party HQ will be the focal point of the administrative machinery, which organizes your party's general election campaigns. The research staff will be based there too. Your party owes it to its active supporters and to itself, as well as to you, to provide the best organization possible and to help draft a manifesto which will convince sufficient numbers of the tens of millions of people whose votes you are seeking. But they know and you know that even the best organization and the most perfect manifesto (neither of which, in the nature of things, is your party likely perpetually to be blessed with) cannot win an election for a government whose policies and actions have not gained sufficient support during a five-year Parlia-

94

ment. To establish close contact between government and party that can help to ensure victory is preferable to recriminations after defeat.

You have fought and won the election that brought to power the government of which you are a member on your party's manifesto, and that in turn was based on a much more detailed programme, worked out during the years of Opposition. Now you have to do your best to carry out that manifesto and abide by the principles of that programme; what is more, you have to be seen to be doing it. It may seem to you unfair that the burden of proof is on you, when day after day in your ministerial life you encounter such formidable difficulties. But you are a volunteer in politics, not a conscript; nobody begged you to sign up. Do not expect those who are outside Parliament fully to understand or to sympathize with the problems of your job: the filibustering in Standing Committee, the difficulties in mustering a majority in the Division Lobby. It is up to you to explain the problems. It is your responsibility, even more, to demonstrate that despite the problems you are doing your best to keep faith. The responsibility for proving that you are not growing remote is yours.

And if keeping in touch with your party is important at all times, it is important most of all when the going gets tough. Not only do your supporters have the right to know the worst, and the reasons why the worst has come about. Their support and understanding at such times can help sustain you. So do not simply wait for your party to come to you for information and explanation. If you take the initiative yourself, you can help to avoid a great deal of misunderstanding.

You may be preoccupied night and day in working to achieve the fulfilment of election commitments. Do not, however, expect the party to be aware of every one of these achievements unless you tell them; so take the trouble to tell them. Remember that as a minister with a great department at his disposal you have access to more information than your party's research department can hope to accumulate. You should share it with them. This may be done through a political adviser appointed by the ministerial head of your department or – if he prefers his ministerial team to be his political advisers – direct to the research staff at your party head-quarters. Of course you must observe the necessary proprieties, and not use public resources for party propaganda. But the Permanent Secretary of your department will in any case be watching to make sure this does not happen; and if you are in any doubt you can consult him.

The Labour Party has always been very cautious about how when in office it copes with the relationship between government and party. Represented by its opponents as the party which, if only at the back of its mind, is revolutionary in intention, Labour has tended to behave much more conventionally than the Conservatives. More often than not the Chairman of the Conservative Party, the head of its organization outside Parliament, has been a member of the Cabinet and privy to all the government's secrets. On the contrary the Labour Party, as a result of unsatisfactory experiences in its early days when its General Secretary could be an active career politician, does not now even permit him to sit in the House of Commons. The Rule Book of the party lays down specifically: 'The General Secretary . . . shall devote his or her whole time to the work of the party and shall not be eligible to act as a parliamentary candidate.' It has sometimes seemed to me that this rule should be changed and that when a Labour government is in office the General Secretary should automatically be made a member of the Cabinet or, at very least, appointed to the Privy Council so that the Prime Minister may give him confidential information protected by the Privy Councillor's oath.

This gap in communication means that ministers must strive hard to keep in contact with party headquarters and the National Executive Committee. Of course the Prime Minister and other ministers who happen to be members of the NEC are well placed to do this. However, just because you are not a member of the NEC, this does not mean that you are absolved from the effort. You will find it useful to hold periodic meetings at your department with the full-time staff of party headquarters, to share your information and your intentions with them, and what is more to seek their advice too. All party research staffs – like all ministerial teams – are variable in quality; some, however, can be very good indeed, and you may be lucky. At very least no one can accuse you of not trying.

Of course your party headquarters must try too; this is not a one-way traffic. And along the way you may have some wry experiences. The 1978 Labour Party Conference debated several important resolutions relevant to the work of the Department of Industry, passing two of these resolutions and remitting a third for further consideration by the National Executive Committee. The National Executive in its turn asked for a meeting with the department's ministers to discuss the resolutions, and the Secretary of State immediately agreed. A date and time were arranged and, in a Conference Room at the department's Victoria Street offices (only a few minutes' walk away both from the Houses of Parliament and the then Party headquarters), the ministers at the department, in company with the Secretary of State for Employment and Civil Service officials, awaited the large and formidable contingent from the National Executive who had communicated their intention of turning up. But only three, one of whom was the youthful representative of the Young Socialists, actually arrived; one of these three was very late and another left early. The meeting proceeded all the same, but the story got around and the weekly *Tribune* severely criticized the National Executive for its laxness. A second meeting was therefore organized, but the attendance was little better. As an exercise in discussion and communication it was not the most sensational success, but at any rate the ministers had shown they were willing.

Of course there are periodic meetings held within the party where ministers can attend to put their case. The Labour Party's National Executive spawns a network of subcommittees, which in their turn generate their own subcommittees. At this third level people who are not elected members of the Executive can be co-opted, and it has been the practice when the party is in office that ministers from the departments whose functions are relevant to the work of particular subcommittees are asked to attend. So you will have the opportunity not only to help in the formulation of future party policy (which, if your party wins the next election and you remain at your department, will be the policy you will have to carry out) but also to set the record straight if there are any misunderstandings about what you are doing now.

Of course your party is not simply a London headquarters. It has constituency parties and branches all over the country. There are constituencies represented in Parliament by MPs from your party, and other constituencies which your party has not won, maybe never can win. Believe it or not, party members in these areas will be interested to hear what you have to tell them. You may think, from your elevated position, that ministers are two a penny. But party members do not see them every day of the week. So do your best to accept if your party's Campaigns Officer asks you to address party members in your area, or even farther away. He will ask you very nicely, reporting that he has received a special request for your presence; while sometimes the party concerned may have applied for any minister who is available, sometimes they really will have asked for you. I was on one occasion invited to be guest at a constituency party's annual dinner, and the local MP told me that the invitation had had nothing to do with him but had been decided by a vote of the constituency General Management Committee. Since the constituency in question was Cardiff South-East and the MP James Callaghan I was ready to believe him, particularly since at that time I had responsibility for the steel industry and Cardiff South-East was the location of a major steelworks (later, sadly, shut down).

You do not, though, have to wait for an invitation to visit your party supporters. In the course of your ministerial duties you will travel around the country on official visits. There is no reason why these should not be combined with party Meetings. If you are in Troon to visit a shipyard it is no trouble at all to have a tea meeting at the local hotel with party members. Nor does it do any harm to combine ministerial visits with participation in by-election campaigns. You can get useful publicity which the candidate will not complain about.

Indeed, your presence will be welcomed especially in by-election campaigns. The top Cabinet ministers will of course be the featured attractions in the marginal contests; but in an unwinnable constituency, at a meeting in a village hall where only a handful may attend, they will be glad to see even you. At very least your presence will provide entertainment for the local Young Conservatives. And you can help out not only by addressing meetings but by canvassing and touring working men's clubs too. This will be good for your soul, as well as providing you with needed refreshment.

It is always a good idea to remember that by-elections and local elections are in the offing. Their arrival may even stimulate you into making decisions that have been hanging fire; better still, it may stimulate your ministerial colleagues, in Cabinet or Cabinet Committee assembled, at last to decide in your favour issues for which you have been finding it difficult to obtain consent. All you need to do is to jog their minds. And when decisions are going to be made anyhow, their timing can be of great importance in election campaigns. In 1949 Sir Stafford Cripps, as Chancellor of the Exchequer, brought in an austerity budget in the middle of the elections for the old London County Council; overnight, Labour posters were removed from voters' windows. In 1969 Richard Crossman, by then Secretary of State for Social Services, announced increases in charges for spectacles and dentures a few days before the May local elections. Vast numbers of Labour councillors lost their seats in a landslide against the party. There probably would have been a landslide anyhow, since the government was very unpopular at the time, but the blame fell on Crossman – particularly since, in his almost endearingly frank way, he admitted afterwards that he had forgotten all about the local elections.

This episode came into my mind eight years later, when I was at the Department of Industry with responsibility, among other things, for the Post Office. The Price Commission, in its infinite and impenetrable wisdom, had examined the profits of the Post Office, had come to the conclusion that they were too high, and had therefore decided to use its legal powers to compel the Post Office to refund to customers £100 million of the profits. The Post Office considered how to do this and their Chairman, Sir William Ryland, came to see me at the department, to inform me that his preferred method of repayment would be to make individual rebates to each subscriber. The following Sunday morning, canvassing on a pre-war council house estate in my constituency for the local elections due the next week, I noticed that new telephone directories, being delivered on Sunday mornings in what the Post Office assured me was a cost-effective manner, were sitting on the doorsteps of many houses. This indicated to me that many potential Labour voters were telephone subscribers and consequently eligible for the planned rebates. I therefore saw no reason to object when the announcement about the rebates was made that same week, and conveniently in time for polling day.

The grand finale to the political year is of course the party's annual conference, taking place as it does at the end of the long parliamentary recess in the summer, and just before Parliament reconvenes for the new session. By then you will have had your holiday. But you should give yourself the pleasure of an outing to the seaside, your Party Conference being held as it is either at Brighton or Blackpool. There you can see your own constituency delegate, enjoy your union's social gatherings, and even attend the actual sessions of the Conference itself. Simply by sitting and listening to the debates you can learn a lot about how your party is thinking and feeling. And, though you have to take your chance with everyone else, you even have the opportunity of making a speech. If you are minded, you can tell the Conference about what the government has been doing to carry out its election commitments.

You can also be present to observe the passing of party Conference decisions. Not all Conference decisions become party policy; the party constitution says quite specifically that 'no proposal shall be included in the party programme unless it has been adopted by party conference by a majority of not less than two thirds of the votes recorded on a card vote.' This of course does not necessarily mean that the proposal will be included in the party programme even if it does get a two-thirds majority. And even if a decision is included in the programme, it will not necessarily find its way into the election manifesto. Even so, Conference decisions must receive serious consideration by a Labour government.

Over the years there has been a great deal of earnest and concerned discussion within the Labour Party as to whether Conference decisions should be regarded as binding upon a Labour government, individual ministers, or back-bench Members of Parliament. Of course, Labour ministers would have found it convenient for MPs to be bound by Conference decisions in the late 1960s, when the Party Conference repeatedly endorsed the then Labour government's statutory incomes policies, against which many back-benchers were in rebellion. It would have been equally useful in the late 1970s, when the Conference again endorsed that Labour government's economic policies in general and its incomes policy specifically, here too despite disagreement from numerous back-benchers. That state of affairs would also have suited the Labour government when in 1967 the party Conference voted to welcome Britain's application to join the Common Market and more than eighty Labour MPs refused to support the application. I must confess that I myself showed my disagreement with a Conference decision when, in defiance of the most recent Conference vote on the subject, I voted in Parliament (in a free vote) in 1976 in favour of a Private Member's Bill to abolish the House of Lords. Understandably, it is the Conference decisions which coincide with our own views that most of us tend to remember. I, for example, am always ready to remind anyone who cares to listen (though my audience gets smaller and smaller) that I had the privilege of piloting through the House of Commons the Act which fulfilled the 1971 Conference decision calling for the nationalization of the shipbuilding industry.

Whether you are able to take account of Conference decisions as conclusively as that, and whether you agree with them or not, you should certainly pay due heed to them. The 1978 Conference passed a resolution calling for the nationalization of a small shiprepair yard on Merseyside, Western Shiprepairers Ltd. The Labour government had no statutory powers to do this. However, as soon as I got back from Blackpool, where the resolution had been passed, I entered into consultations to see if Western Shiprepairers could be taken over by agreement. I failed, and most unhappily the yard closed; but at least I had tried. The same Conference carried a resolution which applauded a plan that shop stewards at Lucas Aerospace had worked out for new projects by their company, and which asked the government to take steps to forward the implementation of this plan. Since the company was privately owned there were limits to what the government could do. However, spurred on by the Conference resolution, I took initiatives which eventually led to a meeting under my chairmanship, involving the shop stewards, their union leaders and the Lucas Aerospace management, at which the management agreed to set up a joint working party with the unions to see whether any of the stewards' plans could be implemented. It was, at any rate, progress. And the party could see that we had made the effort.

I remember Anthony Crosland – who himself made the most meticulous efforts to maintain contacts with the party – groaning to me: 'I wish they would take account of *our* problems!' And of course I sympathized with him. It is essential that the party should know all you have to put up with, and to understand that ministerial life is not all lunches and trips abroad. But you on your part should appreciate their feelings of frustration and their impatience. That is what a dialogue is all about. Make sure you keep your side of it going.

12

How to Work with Outside Interests

———

It will not only be politicians and civil servants who share your ministerial life with you. There will be many outside bodies and individuals – some closely linked with you, others wishing to create links – with whom you will have to work. Some will be bodies which you yourself set up, such as committees of inquiry. Governments somewhat at a loss as to what to do about a problem tend to resort to setting up a committee to inquire into it. Some of these committees, like the housing finance review established by Anthony Crosland when he was Secretary of State for the Environment and continued by Peter Shore, may be bodies internal to the department and entirely within your control.

Others may be Quangos – quasi-autonomous non-governmental organizations. Such bodies have always been a device of government but eventually, particularly through the energetic efforts of a Conservative Member of Parliament called Philip Holland, came to be associated with the alleged excesses and inefficiencies of socialism. Holland, an amiable man, was much offended when I accused him, as Chairman of the Committee of Selection which nominated the members of a medley of new House of Commons Select Committees, of being an arch-creator of Quangos. Be that as it may, pick up the newspaper any day and you will see that another Quango has been created. At the Department of the Environment there were two in which I was closely involved. One, run jointly with the Department of Industry, was the Waste Management Advisory Council, a body established to further such worthy devices as recycling discarded rubbish and putting it to fresh and constructive uses. I was not too thrilled with the idea of Quangos myself and failed to respond with joy when asked to accept the joint chairmanship of this body but – as so often in my ministerial life –

had to succumb; rather flatteringly, or else in sheer desperation, the Council itself insisted on it.

The other Quango, the London Housing Action Group, was created by the 1970–4 Conservative government. I inherited its chairmanship from my Tory predecessor at the Department of the Environment, and at its meetings not only learned valuable lessons about housing in London but also gained a new insight into the, for me as a provincial MP, perplexing nature of politics in the capital. I discovered that the normal, or at any rate expected, party antagonism between Labour and Conservative (both represented on the Group) was as nothing to the hostility verging on loathing that could exist – not of course on a personal basis – between the London boroughs and the Greater London Council. Socialists representing the boroughs would be at the throats of their fellow socialists from the GLC while Conservatives, instead of staying on the sidelines and enjoying the fun, ferociously joined in, the borough Tories siding with the borough socialists against members of their own party foolish enough to be associated with the detested GLC. Despite these ever-looming antagonisms the Group did produce very useful reports. However, dealing with that little lot gave me a keen sympathetic insight into the travails of Henry Kissinger, who only had the Arabs and Israelis to cope with.

Almost every minister in every department has his ration of such bodies with which he is required to deal. I inherited membership of a beauty, to do with defence materials procurement, when I went to the Department of Industry. But these are only the tip of the iceberg. Nearly all government departments, in addition, now have their links with or outright responsibilities for public bodies of one kind or another, whether the National Health Service (Department of Health and Social Security), or the local authorities (Departments of the Environment, and Education and Employment).

Then there are the Next Steps agencies, more than a hundred bodies ranging from the Prison Service to the National Weights and Measures Laboratory, to which government departments have hived off huge chunks of their administrative activities and two-thirds of their staff (the latter, either to their satisfaction or their embarrassment, sometimes compulsorily garbed in 'corporate clothing'). There are, in addition, a forlorn handful of surviving nationalized industries, such as the Post Office and British Coal.

You will discover that these agencies and industries are shared out, like so many toffees, between different government departments, who are regarded as having total control of them though, fortunately or unfortunately, having no such thing. You will share – or even shoulder entirely – the responsibility for appointing the chairmen and chief executives of the organizations for which your department is responsible. You will be required by Parliament to receive their annual reports. You will examine their development plans, scrutinize their finances (in many cases being their only financier), claim a dividend from their profits or fund their losses, and have the right, sometimes statutory, sometimes agreed with them informally, to vet and approve certain of their major investment projects. You will meet their chairmen and other leading functionaries regularly.

It is they who will be responsible for managing their organizations, but it is you who, however indignantly or lachrymosely, will be left holding the exploding parcel when – as they undoubtedly and inexorably will – things go wrong. When so many escapes took place from prisons that it began to seem that incarceration in these allegedly impregnable establishments was optional and subject to the consent of the inmates, the Home Secretary argued that such unlicenced excursions were matters of administration, for which the head of the Prison Service was responsible, rather than policy, which comprised the Home Secretary's domain. After Parliament nevertheless insisted that he himself was responsible, the Home Secretary discharged that responsibility by discharging the head of the Prison Service (who, having been deprived of a salary substantially larger than the Home Secretary's, had to make do with compensation that would not have been sneezed at by a National Lottery prize winner).

Ministers are paid far less not only than many heads of Quangos whom they appoint, but less even than a substantial number of the civil servants with whom they deal daily. A department of Industry messenger, serving tea to an inter-departmental meeting of civil servants over whom I happened to be presiding, spilled a full cup down the collar of one of the officials (an Under-Secretary, I believe). He – the messenger that is, the official having been trained to maintain a stiff upper lip under whatever trying circumstances – was so overcome with remorse that, to assuage his feelings, I pointed out that the official would be able to send the garment to be cleaned and added, 'After all, he is paid more than I am.' Thinking the matter over further, I went on: 'In fact every official in this room is paid more than I am.' Afterwards my Private Secretary, as Private Secretaries should, corrected an error I had made. He told me that there were in fact two people in the room who were not paid more than I. All the same, ministers – as this book illustrates – have other consolations apart from pay. Industrialists, on the other hand, are really quite interested in their salaries and even more in their pensions.

Anthony Crosland blackmailed one socialist whom he was seeking to appoint to the chairmanship of a nationalized industry, and who very validly pointed to the financial sacrifice he would have to make if he accepted, by telling him that it was time he did something for socialism; it was an effective ploy, and it worked. I myself was able to attempt a variation of this approach when, at the Department of Industry, I called in a group of shipping owners who were contemplating placing an order in Japan rather than Sunderland. They put up all kinds of arguments as to why this was a sensible course for them to take. I countered with the only really strong argument I had available, an appeal to their patriotism. They asked for a few minutes to consider this novel line of argument, and then came back into the room to tell me they accepted it. Their ships were built in Sunderland, and they were later kind enough to write and tell me how pleased they were with them.

You will find the heads of industries and agencies with whom you deal a mixed lot, resembling each other only in their dedication to the organizations they manage. Often they have taken on the positions through a genuine urge to serve their country. You will find that if any of them are actually ex-ministers, possibly having held your own job, to achieve the right note in your relationship may be difficult, since they may with justice regard you as a jumped-up upstart not fit for the position they graced. Lord Beswick, whom I replaced as Minister of State at the Department of Industry with responsibility for the aircraft industry when he was appointed Chairman-designate of British Aerospace, never gave the slightest hint that he felt this way and throughout treated me with great courtesy; but I was always conscious that he might be thinking superior thoughts, and was accordingly galvanized into doing my very best.

Lord Beswick was indeed a man of sterling mettle, as he proved on one occasion by seriously disconcerting the Duke of Edinburgh. The Duke was guest of honour at a lunch at the Farnborough Air Show held while the nationalization Bill was going through Parliament, and was seated at a circular table with Lord Beswick placed, very appropriately as it turned out, tangentially to him. The Duke expressed views about nationalization of the aircraft industry which could be taken as endearing or infuriating depending on your point of view. There was no doubting Lord Beswick's point of view, and he snapped at the Duke so fiercely that His Royal Highness was quite taken aback. The Duke, of course, is famed for his plain speaking as I myself discovered when, after lining up for half an hour in freezing snowy weather prior to the royal opening of the Birmingham National Exhibition Centre, I was eyed by him as he came down the line and asked, with no convincing answer evidently expected: 'What are you doing here?' This might of course have been because he had no idea who on earth I was.

Tom King, who was for a time a Conservative spokesman on industry and attacked me in the 1979 election campaign for allegedly having had no experience of industry (he later became Minister of State for Local Government without having had any experience in local government) once accused the Labour government of conducting its relationships with nationalized industries by means of the 'lunch-time nudge'. Even if your views on official lunches are the same as mine, you will find yourself occasionally obliged to accept hospitality from the organizations you sponsor. I went to lunch in this way with the directors of Cable and Wireless, then a wholly government-owned Companies Act company and one of the country's oldest and most successful public sector businesses. I congratulated them on being a credit to state ownership, but they confessed that they rather liked to keep dark their nationalized status in order not to put off foreign customers. I remembered this discussion rather wryly when, in trying to persuade the Saudi Arabian Minister of Telephones to consider Cable and Wireless as the organizer of a communications consortium in his country, I received the response that he would have more faith in a publicly owned body.

You will learn a great deal about management style and even more about human nature from your contacts with the heads of the organizations you sponsor. I, for example, discovered that Bob Scholey, a Yorkshireman known as Black Bob by the workers in the steel industry during his period as the Corporation's Deputy Chairman, went weak at the knees at the sound of Richard Strauss's *Der Rosenkavalier*. You will be impressed by the sheer scale of the knowledge of his industry of a man like Sir William Ryland, who had worked his way up within the Post Office before becoming its chairman. You will be overwhelmed by the devastating courtesy (though with steel concealed inside) of one such as Sir Anthony Griffin, first Chairman of British Shipbuilders who, during the interminable parliamentary proceedings on the nationalization Bill, could be seen constantly in the Commons gallery witnessing the snail's progress towards the Statute Book. When during the Report Stage of the Bill an Opposition spokesman accused Sir Anthony of having insufficient experience of maritime matters I read out his entry in *Who's Who*:

> *Educ*: RN Coll., Dartmouth. Joined RN, 1934; to sea as Midshipman, 1939; War Service in E Indies, Mediterranean, Atlantic, N Russia and Far East; specialised in navigation, 1944; Staff Coll., 1952; Imp. Defence Coll., 1963; comd HMS Ark Royal, 1964–65; Asst Chief of Naval Staff (Warfare), 1966–68; Flag Officer, Second-in-Command, Far East Fleet, 1968–69; Flag Officer, Plymouth, Comdr Central Sub Area, Eastern Atlantic, and Comdr Plymouth Sub Area, Channel 1969–71; Controller of the Navy, 1971–75, Comdr 1951; Capt. 1956; Rear-Adm. 1966; Vice-Adm. 1968; Adm., 1971.

Looking up at the gallery, where of course he was as ever sitting, I thought I detected a minute smile on his modest countenance.

You will learn, too, how adaptable people can be if circumstances require it. Because the nationalization Bill took so very long to enact, Graham Day, the Chief Executive-designate of British Shipbuilders, resigned in understandable impatience. A Civil Service Under-Secretary, Mike Casey, was chosen at short notice to succeed him, and instantly transformed himself from an able functionary into a dynamic tycoon.

Ministers have varying powers over their administrative offspring, ranging from total control to infuriated impotence. You will, however, find that provided you are reasonable, even the most autonomous organizations will take account of your views without surrendering their own independence. Sir William Barlow, Ryland's successor as Chairman of the Post Office, was a tough man of great integrity. Nevertheless, if he had a convincing case put to him, he would without any further argument abandon a project simply because he was capable very quickly of understanding that, in an organization like the Post Office which is constantly in the public eye, something that might make commercial sense could arouse more political problems than it was worth. And he did not have to be nudged, either at the lunch table or anywhere else.

You will find that your sponsorship of publicly owned industries will bring through your door a procession of private industrialists whose businesses depend on orders from the public sector. The staunch defenders of private enterprise who run the major firms engaged in the manufacture of telecommunications equipment were capable of demanding, when BT was part of the Post Office and thus a public sector enterprise, that in order to give them business I should force the Post Office to order equipment it did not need. Steel-plant manufacturers, similarly hardened advocates of private ownership, pleaded for an increase in the British Steel Corporation's investment programme. Sometimes these representations may lead to paradoxical situations. You may find yourself confronted by a deputation of manufacturers of electronic goods making a highly effective case for government intervention to assist their industry; none more so than their association's chairman who, seeing nothing strange in it, will then presently turn up at another conference which spends much of its time denouncing government intervention in industry, he being also the Chairman of the Conservative Party.

It will indeed be quite a relief for you when an industrialist comes to see you without asking for anything. I once had a highly agreeable visit from Sir Freddie Laker who spent much of the time engrossingly describing to me various plans he had, all of them involving the accumulation of large profits for himself, and ended his recital with the words: 'I suppose that sounds very right wing to you?' I replied that it was a great relief to be in the company of someone who had not come whining to a Labour government for public money prior to making a substantial donation to Conservative Party funds.

You will of course have dealings with people who make no bones about wishing to thwart you politically. Though I never actually formally met him (I once bumped into him, literally, in the Central Lobby of the House of Commons, but we did not exchange greetings) I was involved for quite a time in a Holmes-Moriarty confrontation – cast the roles as you please – with Christopher Bailey, chairman of a small shiprepair company in South Wales called Bristol Channel Ship Repairers Ltd. Christopher Bailey's company was included in the list of shiprepairers to be nationalized by our legislation and he was determined to prevent this. He launched a giant public relations campaign, and by providing information about a form of industrial democracy apparently in operation at his establishments sought to persuade Labour MPs to support him, recognizing that a Labour government with hardly any majority in Parliament was vulnerable to defections. Several Labour MPs were indeed for a time convinced of the validity of his case and put their names to an amendment which would have excluded Bristol Channel from the Bill; later they changed their minds, and the legislation passed through the Commons intact.

Bailey had, however, already set experts to scrutinizing the Bill not for policy inadequacies but for technical defects and, much to the chagrin of Department of Industry officials, not to mention ministers, he found one. This held the Bill up, but only for a time. Bailey then sent a representative to warn me, most courteously, that there were plenty more defects where that came from, and that it would save the government a lot of time to remove shiprepair from the Bill. We persisted; he was as good as his word. More defects were indeed alleged, and the House of Lords committed the Bill to a dreaded band of Examiners. These, after prolonged inquiry, found that there were in fact certain defects, very few and not very serious, but enough. I, who for some reason had been regarded as being in personal combat with Bailey, was the one who in the end, to save the Bill as a whole, recommended the exclusion of the shiprepair companies from nationalization. It was without doubt a remarkable victory for Bailey and showed what can be achieved by dogged persistence with the resources, where needed, to back it up. You should never underestimate determined pressure groups.

Some of the groups who ask to see you will have a somewhat less direct stake than Christopher Bailey in seeking to change your policy. They will include bodies like the self-appointed Mail Users' Association, an organization established to secure better and cheaper postal services which, among other advantages, would assist the businesses of those involved in the Association. There will also be other organizations like the Friends of the Earth, who are just plain old altruists anxious to do their fellow citizens a good turn.

Outside organizations over whom you will decidedly have no control at all will be foreign countries. Their ambassadors will call upon you to present invitations to visit their homelands, with consequences to be described in Chapter 15. But there will also be trade negotiations conducted between companies in Britain and foreign countries in which those countries will seek your inter-vention (so will the home-based companies, for details of which see Chapter 14) under the misunderstanding, sometimes deliberately assumed, that the British government is passionately anxious to secure better terms for the foreign customer even at the expense of home manufacturers. Your slightest act can be subtly interpreted in such circumstances. Attendance at, say, a reception at the Finnish Embassy leads to murmured speculation in the chanceries and no doubt to telegrams to Helsinki which, couched as they will be in the world's most impenetrable language, will not even have to be in code.

To all of these – Quangos, agencies, nationalized industries, interest groups, ambassadors of foreign trading partners – you in your turn will have to be a kind of ambassador. It will be your job to represent your government and to prove if at all possible that you are reasonable people without horns or tails, ready to listen to reason and to respond reasonably, without being pliable or unprincipled.

13

How to Work with the Unions

There are those who believe that between 1970 and 1979 three British governments were brought down by the trade unions. There is no doubt at all that confrontation with the unions destroyed Edward Heath's government in February 1974. It is certainly true, as well, that differences with the trade unions over fundamental issues – reform of the unions themselves in 1969, incomes policy in 1978–9 – contributed to the downfall of two Labour governments. Much of the power of the trade unions in national affairs as well as in industry was eroded or even eliminated by a series of Bills enacted during Margaret Thatcher's period of office. Their authority and influence within the Labour Party were reduced under two successive leaders: tentatively by John Smith, decisively by Tony Blair.

Even so, it still makes sense for governments and unions to work together. The unions represent many millions of organized workers; their assistance can eliminate problems which might have caused trouble and make easier for governments the solution of problems that do arise, while their opposition may make existing difficulties worse and create confrontations that co-operation could have prevented altogether. You as a minister can play your part in bringing about the closer understanding that is valuable regardless of the politics of the government in power. If you are a minister in a Labour government you will of course know of the special links that many unions have with your party: the affiliations at national and local level, the financial contributions, the fact that they helped to form the party in the first place.

Remember, too, that as a minister you will be an employer of trade unionists. Your civil servants will be members of some of the most active and articulate unions in the country. So you can start by being a good employer. In doing so you may come across some remarkable practices. The Department of the Environment used to be the sponsoring Department for the Property Services Agency, a body which, set up by a Conservative government, was one of the world's largest organizations for constructing buildings and managing them when built. This agency employed not only white-collar workers, but blue-collar trade unionists too. Ron Brown, a sponsored member of the Furniture, Timber and Allied Trades Union, was the natural and appropriate MP to bring to see me, when I had responsibility for the PSA, employees within the agency who had a grievance to discuss. When they arrived we were, however, unable to get on with discussing the grievance because Ron Brown first had a different grievance to raise with me. He told me that the workers in the deputation were having their pay docked for the time they were spending with me. I found it necessary to bring the meeting to an abrupt halt until I received an assurance from management – of whom I was the ministerial head – that the workers would receive their full pay. So – and this applies to others besides ministers – make sure that you are a good employer yourself before lecturing others on how to achieve better labour relations.

You of course will be in a position to help the unions; but in your turn you may need their help. So the first rule is, see them without hesitation when they ask to meet you on matters they regard as important. Edward Heath's Conservative government might have survived long after 1974 if its Secretaries of State for Trade and Industry had had regular routine meetings with the National Union of Mineworkers well before trouble broke out. You cannot suddenly construct a close and trusting relationship during a crisis. The unions, you may be sure, will want to see you about all manner of issues. They will wish to discuss with you questions of pay in organizations for which you are a sponsoring minister. You can of course get all stuffy and refuse to see them, on the valid grounds that pay negotiations are a matter between them and the employing organization, publicly or privately owned. All this is quite true and it would indeed be a serious error for you to get involved in the actual negotiations or be regarded as a court of appeal against the employer. But even if your government is not trying to run a public sector pay policy there can be no harm in your hearing the unions' grievances and problems, and seeing if you can offer helpful advice.

The unions may ask to see you about preventing closures in their industry. Often the closures cannot be stopped. I was visited at very short notice by the leaders of the Confederation of Shipbuilding and Engineering Unions – the meeting taking place in my cramped and tiny temporary room in the Cabinet Office late one evening – about the threatened closure of Falmouth shiprepair yard; I had a much more formal meeting at the Department of Industry about the closure of Western Shiprepairers. Neither meeting contributed to a successful outcome. The unions' leaders were, however, truthfully able to tell their members that they had tried every possible way of saving their jobs: very important when one of the major problems in trade unionism in recent years has been to maintain links between the national leaders and the rank and file. Indeed, the CSEU leadership brought the Western shop stewards with them and left them to do much of the talking.

The unions will want to see you about getting work for their members. They may come with the telecommunications equipment manufacturers and argue a much more effective case than the employers themselves. They may seek orders for shipyards or new projects for aircraft factories. Their profound knowledge of their industries can only add to your own knowledge as a minister of how to approach the problems of those industries.

There may be special issues on which you can help. The experiment in industrial democracy in the Post Office was launched after great difficulty. The unions faced an employer less hostile than unimaginative. The employer, when he decided at the government's request to accept the experiment in principle, faced unions which were circumscribed by specific decisions made at their delegate conferences. Each found it easier to accept a compromise proposed by an arbitrating minister than to yield a point to their adversary in the negotiations. It was therefore necessary for me, as the minister most closely involved, to seek to construct formulae acceptable to both participants, and this I managed to do. If the Conservative government which later came to power had been willing to play a similar catalytic role, the experiment could have continued instead of being left to wither away. What nearly caused the original experiment to founder before it had been launched was the attitude of one in particular of the smaller unions, which sought representation on the Post Office Board far greater than it had the right to expect in relation to the size of its membership. The union came to me and I readily saw its representatives, but made clear that I could and would accept only a solution arrived at by the unions themselves. It then went to the Liberals, without whose consent the legislation enabling the experiment could not be introduced, but they were wary; it next went to the Conservatives and they too stood at a distance. In the end the experiment was launched with represen- tation for this union as agreed between all the unions involved.

This perplexing episode confirmed for me a lesson that I had begun to learn much earlier and which, if you are not to walk through a political minefield, you must learn too. As a politician you must not interfere in relationships between unions and within unions. If you do you will meet the fate of the person who takes sides in a quarrel between a married couple: when they make up their quarrel they will both turn on you.

You will find it especially necessary to be careful in your relation- ships with shop stewards. One senior minister in the 1974-9 Labour government, with very little knowledge or experience of working-class life, was so enchanted with the very idea of shop stewards that he saw groups of them at his departmental head- quarters whenever they asked to see him and was even rumoured to have a special room set aside for them. Whether this was indeed true, we ministers at the Department of Industry had it made clear to us by the national leadership of the unions with which we were involved that it would be deeply resented if we saw groups of shop stewards at our department without their agreement. This may be regarded as wise or restrictive on their part, but it was for them to decide who was properly representative of their unions.

This problem of relationships between union leaders and their shop stewards was one of the complicating factors in the long story of the attempts to make progress on the corporate plan for Lucas Aerospace compiled by an informal group of shop stewards in that company. The shop stewards won tremendous support, including that of a group of Members of Parliament, but their unions were adamant that any discussions about Lucas Aerospace must take place within what they insisted were their own internal democratic structures. As one very left-wing leader of one of the most left-wing unions put it to me: 'I'm having no rank-and-fileism in my union.' The unions had banned direct contact between the Lucas Aerospace management and the shop stewards' combine and the matter was only resolved, after a series of private meetings in which I was involved, when the shop stewards were included in an official team set up by the Confederation of Shipbuilding and Engineering Unions. Of course this does not mean that the unions can, will, or have the right to place a ban on your seeing shop stewards at all. You will certainly meet them (see Chapter 15) when you visit factories. And it is open to Members of Parliament to include them in delegations of constituents whom they bring to see you (Chapter 14).

You should not, however, imagine that it will always be the unions who will be coming to you for favours. Situations may arise in which you need their help or advice. Sometimes it will assist you in dealing with a delicate or dangerous situation if you have consulted the unions in advance and gained their agreement. During the crisis over Chrysler at the end of 1975 Eric Varley, as Secretary of State for Industry, had frequent meetings with Jack Jones, Hugh Scanlon and others, and was confident of their support for his preferred solution.

You will need the unions' help in industrial difficulties. You will need it, too, in working out details of your own policies, as with the scheme for redundancy payments in shipbuilding (their co-operation in which was a major concession from trade unionists whose official policy was opposition to any compulsory redundancies). You will need it, as well, in assessing your approach to much wider long-term policies for entire industries. The long process by the 1974 Labour government of working out a policy for the steel industry was greatly assisted by consultation with the unions concerned. This does not mean your giving the unions a veto on your policies; sometimes you will have to stand firm on matters they find difficult to accept. It does mean that the co-operation of unions and workforce will make it easier for you to bring about constructive changes in industry.

And there may be times when the goodwill you have built up will be very helpful to you personally or politically. When Eric Varley and I had our difficulties with the Select Committee on National-ized Industries, following the reports they published on the British Steel Corporation, the support we received from the steel unions themselves and from the Scottish Trades Union Congress was very important in demonstrating to Labour Members of Parliament that the Select Committee might be mistaken and we might be right.

The unions also came to our help in a wider and longer-lasting political ordeal, the tormented passage of the Aircraft and Ship-building Industries Act 1977. The vote in Parliament in the first of the debates on the technical shortcomings which had been dis-covered in the Bill, as a result of Christopher Bailey's taking a magnifying glass to its contents, was regarded as hanging by a hair's breadth. The Scottish TUC sent telegrams to the eleven Scottish Nationalist MPs asking them to support the Labour government; but the SNP members refused, not only voting against the govern-ment but tearing up the telegrams publicly on the floor of the House of Commons. The government won by a single vote but this result was disputed, and the vote was taken again some days later. This time the SNP abstained, helping the government to an easy victory. Superficially this was due to an arrangement that I had negotiated with the SNP; but I was sure that without the pressure exerted by trade union support that arrangement would not have been pos-sible. And certainly when, some months later, yet another procedural motion had to be carried to allow the Bill to proceed further, the SNP did not oppose us even though no arrangement had been negotiated. The incident of the tearing-up of the telegrams was never forgotten in Scotland, and was thought to have been a factor in the decline of the SNP in Labour areas.

You cannot get this kind of support from the unions without having built up a strong relationship with them long before you imagined you might need such support. One factor will be your readiness, which should be automatic, to see their leaders whenever they feel it necessary. Sometimes very private meetings with just one or two leaders can be particularly helpful. It was informal meetings which helped to secure even the limited progress that was achieved on the Lucas Aerospace shop stewards' plan.

We made very great progress in dealing with the problems of a much bigger industry by meetings we held with one of its union leaders so private that ministers arranged them personally without their Private Offices knowing about them. This way the meetings did not appear on our diaries, which were circulated widely throughout the department and elsewhere, and there was therefore no question of their existence, let alone what took place at them, leaking out. One very senior minister from outside our department also attended these meetings, and between us we were able during the meetings to clear away bureaucratic obstructions to plain speaking. This did not mean that the union leader sold out his members to us; far from it, he was often very tough. But when a meeting ended we knew exactly where we were with him, how far he thought he could carry his members, what concessions we would have to make, and what we could do with his agreement or tacit assent. Because of these meetings we worked out a viable policy for his industry of great benefit to thousands of the union leader's own members. If you can build up trust of this kind you have created a precious commodity. It means that you can pick up a telephone when you need something and ask for it without any tentative preliminaries while you feel your way. It means that the unions' leaders can do the same. And you need not even have to do it very often.

The winter strikes in early 1979 had a damaging effect on the Labour party's electoral prospects but an effect on daily life and on the economy far more limited than might have been supposed from publicity given to some of the few ugly incidents in those strikes. If some of these disputes had escalated, and if some had broken out which were prevented, the effect on the country could have been catastrophic, as I know from my weeks in the Cabinet Office. That this did not happen is to a large extent due to the liaison built up between ministers in several departments and the leaders of the unions concerned. Those leaders included some trade unionists depicted at the time as extremists.

Trade unionism has had its bad periods in Britain but, far more often than not, it has been a force for sanity. You can help to harness that force. You cannot do it by standing back and saying that problems are nothing to do with you even if indeed you have no direct involvement. If that is your attitude, join a monastic order rather than a government. However, if you are in politics, make sure that you are on good terms with the unions connected with your departmental work. By doing so you may achieve successes that otherwise would have eluded you. And you may avoid disasters that no one will ever know might have happened.

14

How to Receive Delegations

———

You cannot keep the outside world away from your department. In fact after a time you may begin to consider fitting your office with a revolving door in order to facilitate the arrival (and, in some cases even more devoutly, the departure) of visitors. Indeed, if that was your particular addiction, you could spend your entire time receiving delegations to the exclusion of all other activities.

Some groups who come to London you will meet informally as a favour to a fellow Member of Parliament. A colleague will tell you that he has a group of workers down from his constituency, and would be grateful if you would drop into the Strangers' Bar where he is giving them a drink. The Strangers' Bar is the one drinking place in the Houses of Parliament where Members may freely take visitors and which actually resembles a pub. It is also a centre of rather incompetent intrigue. Alternatively an MP may simply have gathered some constituents together in the Central Lobby of the House, and ask you to spare a moment to go out and see them. This too is a painless favour, although it does mean running the gauntlet of certain regular visitors to the Central Lobby, including the man who for many years has waited patiently there for the Prime Minister to send out a message with the news that at last a peerage is to be conferred upon him.

However, the place where people really want to come and put their troubles (or ideas) to you is your own department; for some, nowhere else will really do. Certain would-be visitors will have to be seen, whatever your feelings about them or their objective in coming. You should make it a rule, as practically (though not quite) all ministers do automatically, to agree to see any Member of Parliament who asks to see you, regardless of party or reason. Never forget that the supreme authority of this country is not the government but Parliament, and that election confers a status on a person who, possibly (but surely not) quite undistinguished otherwise, has been chosen to represent tens of thousands of his fellow citizens.

While many MPs will be perfectly happy to come and see you on their own or together with parliamentary colleagues, others will want to bring delegations with them. It is for you to decide whether such a delegation is acceptable. You may well make it a rule to see any delegation which an MP from your own party wishes to bring, while considering any other MP's delegation on the merits of the subject it wishes to raise. However, even when an MP from your own party is involved, there may be a problem; he may be not only an MP, but a fellow minister. When recent Labour governments have been in office, the Prime minister has laid it down that ministers must not take part in public representations to other ministers. But ministers are MPs too, with constituents to pacify and one eye always on the next election; and constituents cannot be expected to preoccupy themselves with rules laid down by Prime Ministers. They want to see their own MP in action. The MP-minister cannot ask parliamentary questions or raise constituency issues in parliamentary debate. Some years ago, a government Whip – and remember, government Whips are not even allowed to make speeches, except along the lines of 'I beg to move this House do now adjourn' – asked Harold Wilson's permission to raise constituency issues in adjournment debates. He was gently refused, but he may have had a point. So, with all these other limitations, exclusion from deputations, despite the obvious need for a minister not to be seen publicly questioning his own government's policies, is a serious deprivation. Conducting all his constituency business in Parliament by way of correspondence is scarcely an adequate substitute.

You will want to help (after all, you may at some time need similar help yourself) and it is possible for you to devise an acceptable formula. The minister can arrive in your office with his delegation. He can bring with him an MP from a nearby constituency to do the actual talking. There is then no reason why the minister should not introduce the members of the delegation to his ministerial colleague and then either withdraw altogether or sit at the end of the table in silence (an occasional meaningful clearing of the throat being accepted as silence). When you have seen Cabinet ministers wait in this way upon members of the government much their junior, you will agree that political conventions can be hard taskmasters. Such situations can also offer illuminating insights into ministerial idiosyncrasies. When a delegation of aircraft workers from Bristol asked to meet me at the Department of Industry I assented readily, assenting equally readily to the request of Tony Benn, then a Bristol MP, to accompany his constituents as a silent invigilator. Benn at the time was Secretary of State for Energy and, at a judiciously chosen time prior to the meeting, a uniformed messenger from the Department of Energy arrived at the Department of Industry ceremonially bearing the ministerial tea mug.

Members of Parliament seek to bring delegations to see ministers for a wide variety of reasons. One reason, not to be sneered at, is simply to show constituents that their MP can get them in to see a minister. Another cause may be the inability of the constituents to get in to see the minister in any other way. It may well be, too, that the constituents have the expertise to explain a problem or issue to a minister in a way that the MP himself cannot. Or the MP may wish the minister to see that an issue on which he has been pressing him is one that arouses strong feeling locally; and politically unsophisticated or inexperienced people can, regrettable though the MP may think it, often convey enthusiasm or anguish better than an eloquent politician. Sometimes the issue may be of such great dimensions that several MPs will bring along a large, mixed deputation including trade unionists, businessmen and local councillors.

Of course there are certain kinds of delegations which, with or without a Member of Parliament, you will always be ready to see. There will be workers worried about their jobs and their future. There will be people who have ideas for projects which might benefit the country, increase exports and create jobs. One Conservative MP – with whom, previously, I had hardly exchanged a word – several times brought to see me a group of people who had worked out plans for advance production of patrol vessels for export. They were enthusiastic and knowledgeable, and I did all I could to advance their project. A Labour colleague, Ray Fletcher, one of the wittiest and most ingenious of all Members of Parliament, was involved in an endeavour to restore Britain to the leading ranks of manufacturers of airships. It took a meeting with him and his associates for me simply to realize what a problem it was for manufacturers to find a place to house these enormous objects. It seemed to me that Fletcher was seeking to further a charming and peaceful notion. I wish I could have helped more than my limited powers allowed.

When delegations write in asking to see you without the support of a sponsoring Member of Parliament, your Private Secretary will send the letter down to the appropriate policy division for advice. It will then come up in a case folder, with a minutely detailed and generally very acute assessment of the qualities and merits of the applicants, followed by a recommendation. You can never go wrong if you agree to see a delegation whom your cautious officials recommend; and they will generally be equally shrewd in their advice to reject. Sometimes, however, they will be irritating enough to wash their hands of the whole thing, with an aloof statement along the lines of: 'There is no departmental necessity for the Minister to see this delegation, although of course he may have some political reason for doing so.' It was this kind of you-make-your-own-mistakes-chum attitude from officials which led a newly appointed member of Margaret Thatcher's administration to wail to me, over a drink in the Smoking Room: 'I wish they'd tell me what to do instead of giving me both sides of the argument!' Of course you, when seeing delegations or in any other of your ministerial activities, will always make up your own mind regardless of the advice of officials.

So whom will you see? Representatives from the Quangos for which you are responsible, of course. Trade Unions, equally certainly, both singly and in groups, such as the Scottish TUC. Joint delegations of workers and management should always be seen; if they can actually get together for something, it must be urgent. One of the most impressive delegations I ever saw was from the whole community of Greenock, including local priests. Greenock had been visited by a calamity. In the community in Great Britain most dependent on shipbuilding their yard, Scott Lithgow, had been afflicted by the collapse of a company called Maritime Fruit Carriers, which had left Scotts building two huge vessels with no customer to accept them. The pleas of the delegation were powerful, and resulted in the first use by the government of its newly established intervention (subsidy) fund for shipbuilding.

Trade associations, too, like those electronics people with the versatile Chairman or the Society of British Aerospace Companies, the extremely successful manufacturers of aircraft components, will want not only to discuss crises but to have periodic meetings to take stock. Groupings of like-minded tradesmen, such as those who run car salesrooms, will rush to see you when there is a danger of a car manufacturing group closing down.

Moving on from people like this, who have genuine problems which they have the right to discuss with someone in authority, you will get to the grey area. For there are people who wish to see you whom you probably ought not to see; and others whom you certainly ought not to see. These will be entrepreneurs or businessmen who wish to exploit an encounter with you for monetary gain. The absence of corruption in governments of all parties in Britain can be seriously impaired if some would-be visitors are given the cachet of having been even in the same room with a Minister of the Crown. If you are foolish enough to admit such people, do not be surprised if they turn up with transistorized machines to place your encounter literally on record.

Local authorities – bodies (mostly, give or take a Westminster or two) of undoubted probity – are in a special class of their own when wishing to send delegations to see you. After all they are fellow politicians, and as well as being seriously concerned for their areas they will be watchful of the political nuances as well. Generally all major parties represented on a local authority will make sure they are involved. So you will have to take great care that you are not regarded as over-blatantly favouring the councillors in your own party, particularly if they are not the majority party on the council, while at the same time ensuring that you do not commit the even more heinous sin of favouring the representatives of the opposing party, even if they are in the majority. I did my best not to fall into this trap; it will be held to my credit or discredit, depending upon the point of view, that in the Labour Party in one North-Western town I was still, several years later, almost revered for having put a controlling Conservative group (which simply did not want to build any houses at all) in their place.

At the Department of the Environment I was constantly approached by councils who did want to build houses, but in addition to any other current restrictions were inhibited from doing so by the cost yardstick. Michael Heseltine subsequently abolished this device of monetary control, whose purpose was to ensure that councils did not go in for building luxury accommodation of the kind which became much in demand by investors from the Persian Gulf. During my time at DoE one council certainly did wish to do this, believing that local authority tenants, whom it wished to house in a planned estate to be built adjacent to a millionaire's area tucked away within its boundaries, should not be made to feel inferior to their neighbours. In such cases I hardened my heart. On the whole, though, my own view was that the cost yardstick should be as flexible as was needed to get decent houses built. This may be regarded as having been an easy way to operate a restriction, but cost yardsticks did not house people and houses do.

Of course the Department of the Environment (together with the Scottish and Welsh Offices) is fair game for local authorities wishing to see ministers about practically anything. Other departments will be selected as destinations by councillors – whose invariably vast delegations will generally also include the Town Clerk (or Chief Executive), often Welsh, and the Borough Treasurer (or Director of Finance), invariably bespectacled – for rather more idiosyncratic reasons. The delegation that came to see me from Hull about renewal of their telephone licence walked into my room at the Department of Industry confident in the belief that my consent was cut and dried. They were much perturbed when it was broken to them, in gradual stages to soften the blow, that the issue would be decided on its merits; they had not bargained for that kind of partiality. There were, however, important issues to be considered, including the conflicting attitudes of two important trade unions, and not to mention the question of whether Hull could provide or obtain the resources necessary for essential capital re-equipment. When I told the delegation that to begin with their licence would be renewed only temporarily, they were furious. However, we became good friends, especially when their licence was eventually renewed on a more long-term basis.

Of course, not only delegations from the United Kingdom will wish to see you. It will be firmly borne in upon you that aircraft are landing incessantly at Heathrow with manifests of passengers whose dominating objective in making the trip is to attain a meeting with you in your department; this interview may even have been included as part of a package tour by their travel agent. In such cases the advice will come to you not only from your own department but also from the Foreign Office, who have their own mystic reasons for doing anything. You will be fascinated to learn that for you to decline to see a group of machine-tool manufacturers from Venezuela could have damaging effects (or on the other hand no effect at all) on the balance of power in Latin America. Parts of the world are at any one given time in with the Foreign Office, while other parts are definitely out. You will learn which, when their inhabitants inexplicably seek to enter your presence.

Some delegations from abroad will actually have been incited to come here by invitation of the Foreign Office or of your own or some other department acting on the advice of the Foreign Office. In such cases not only will it be inescapable that you receive them, you may even be strong-armed into going to meet them when they arrive at Heathrow (from which, after a few minutes' uneasy conversation, they will depart by government Daimler for Claridges while you return home to bed, such delegations invariably arriving remarkably early on Sunday mornings).

Groups visiting Britain under official auspices will be preceded into your office by a handsome booklet detailing their programme, which will often give them the benefit of a visit to the steelworks at Scunthorpe as well as an entrée to you. When they arrive they will enter in some style, preceded by an official from the Government Hospitality Department who has seen it all and is still enthusiastic. An official from your own department will also be present whose sole function, so far as you can gather, for you have never seen him fulfil any other, is to sit in complete silence throughout the meeting. In cases where the visitors' language is unusually recondite there will also be interpreters, at least one if not more.

These remarkable people will display their expertise at their incredible craft by jotting down about three words from the speech they are translating and then speaking non-stop for several minutes; in doing so, so far as it is possible for you to gather, they will convey with clinical accuracy to each participant what the other has said. I was always greatly impressed by the single-minded devotion of these interpreters at official dinners. They would sit between me and my principal guest, a few inches to the rear, and zealously toss the conversation back and forth on our behalf while we ate our prawn cocktail (or melon). On one occasion I became disturbed that we were eating and conversing while the interpreter was going hungry, and offered to remain silent for a while so that she could partake of something. She indulgently told me that she had already eaten, a trick of the trade which with a little intelligence I might have thought out for myself.

These delegations from abroad will give fascinating displays of national characteristics (as no doubt you will too): vast parties of courteous Chinese immaculately dressed, though no longer uniformly garbed in Mao suits; equally large posses of equally courteous Japanese, their briefcases apparently but deceptively full of orders for British goods which never seem to materialize in the quantities anticipated; robed Arabs exuding even more exquisite courtesy. Sometimes you will be asked to escort your guests to an entertainment, with the opera or ballet at Covent Garden a choice preferred by officialdom. However, asked themselves to choose, the delegations may opt for something less taxing and more jolly. One requested something along the lines of the Black and White Minstrels and, this entertainment not being currently available at the time, was taken instead to see an excellent all-black show from Broadway called *Bubbling Brown Sugar*. At your initial or final encounter (though preferably not at *Bubbling Brown Sugar*) the Central Office of Information will send along a photographer to memorialize your amity, which very likely will indeed have been genuine; these pictures later to be reproduced in the columns of your departmental magazine.

Your meetings with such groups will proceed according to a ritualistic scenario, to vary which would disturb all participants. Visits of foreign businessmen will, however, be much more routine events. You will try to get them to buy British goods, and they will try to get you to let their products into Britain with fewer restrictions. Representatives from the handful of colonial territories which remain will be much in evidence, their small wants unfortunately often in conflict with the needs of areas in Britain containing disproportionate numbers of marginal constituencies.

It will, though, be those representatives of marginal constituencies from your own Parliamentary Party whom you will wish most to help, and whose delegations you will most seek to impress. Your officials will prepare you well for these meetings. The night before you will find in your box a meetings brief, which will include pocket biographies of all expected participants, details about the area they come from including local industries and unemployment levels, a well presented summary of the problem they wish to discuss, and at the end a 'Line to Take'. You do not have to take this line, and quite often you will not, but your officials will judge your skill in handling the delegation by the extent to which you adhere to their recommended line. When the meeting ends they may be all smiles, or else seeking to repress reproving frowns. Your main objective, as you see it, will be to send the delegation away satisfied, though without having committed yourself to anything inconsistent with the government's stated policies.

Whether they do go away satisfied will depend a great deal on how you handle the meeting. If the delegation you are seeing is introduced by a fellow Member of Parliament, do not let him do all the talking. After all he has constant opportunities, in the Division Lobby and elsewhere, to discuss with ministers whatever he likes. Of course he should demonstrate his right of access to a minister by introducing the members of the delegation and outlining the case they seek to make. It is then a good idea for you to ask the identified lay leader of the group to speak (he will probably have carefully prepared a statement, and may have brought with him written documents to present as well) and then go round the table asking other members of the delegation to add their contributions to the case they seek to make. Do not jump in too early with your own response; after all, you too are not short of opportunities for self-expression. When you do reply be honest. It may well be that you have good news for the delegation, or at any rate can truthfully tell them that your mind is open and that what they have said will be considered carefully; this will probably involve your officials in writing letters to various other ministers or agencies.

If, though, your only genuine response must be to reject their pleas or to admit that there is nothing you can do, then say exactly that, though in language not too brutal to be palatable. It is more cruel to let a delegation go away with falsely based hopes than to tell them the worst. And in case any doubt may remain, whatever the nature of your response, it is a good idea to offer to send the escorting MP a letter setting out what you have said; that way there will be no room for misunderstanding. After you have made your response you should give the delegation a further chance for comment and then allow the sponsoring MP the last word. And when the meeting is over do not appear to be turning your visitors brusquely out of the room. You may be busy (or think you are) but they have come a long way and brought a lot of hope with them.

This kind of procedure, with the necessary variations, can be used as well for delegations which do not include a Member of Parliament. However, whoever they are, whoever brings them and whatever purpose they come for, treat your visitors hospitably. They may be workers who have never even been to London before, let alone come into a government department with its rather formidable paraphernalia of entry passes, security checks, doormen, messengers and Private Secretaries. They may be visitors from abroad who will form their opinion of Britain on the basis of their experience of people like yourself. They may be industrialists of immense power. Whoever they are, give them a cup of tea or coffee and make sure someone has asked them whether they would like to use the cloakroom. Remember how you felt when you were an Opposition back-bencher trying to make a case to a minister from another party. And bear in mind that sooner or later you are likely to be back in that same supplicant position. So do as you would be done by.

15

Have Red Box, Will Travel

Well, not quite; you will not be allowed to take your ministerial red box abroad with you, and you will be unwise to travel in Britain with it. It is heavy and bulky, and it attracts attention. When you need to have government documents with you, it is much more advisable to take with you an anonymous, though government-issue, brown or black leather briefcase. But whatever you do take with you, you will travel.

How often you travel, and how far you go will depend largely on the department to which you are assigned. At the Foreign Office and the Department of Trade and Industry you will need almost an open ticket. At the Northern Ireland Office you will make dozens if not hundreds of journeys across the Irish Sea. Even in the more prosaic departments you will need to visit government installations, hospitals, schools and housing estates in Britain. Sometimes, too, you will be required to travel to other countries and continents, something which some ministers loathe and to which others become addicted.

You will have a variety of reasons for travelling within Britain. Do not, however, give yourself any delusions of grandeur. Only the Prime Minister travels at home in anything resembling style. He or she will have a reserved railway compartment or an aircraft of the Queen's Flight. If the Prime Minister travels by train the station manager will be there to see him off, with another to meet him at the other end. As well as the indispensable Private Secretary he will be accompanied by an assistant from the Garden Room at Number Ten.

There will be nothing like that for you, though. If you are travelling within a reasonable distance from London, you will probably go by your own government car. Your driver will regard your arrival on time as being his personal responsibility and a matter of prestige. Perhaps, on reconsideration, I am doing him an injustice by saying that he will want to get you there on time; he will, in fact, aim to set out so early that if travel conditions are anything at all like normal you will arrive so far ahead of schedule that you will have time to do the journey all over again. As you get near to your destination the car will creep more and more slowly, and your driver's head will hang more and more sheepishly. You will in the end resort to driving in concentric circles around your destination until it is safe to assume that the reception party will be ready on the doorstep for you. On journeys such as this I have seen at leisure some of the most – and also the least – attractive scenic spots in the Home Counties. Your driver will have taken these ludicrous, but to him essential, precautions because he has heard of hold-ups in the traffic bulletins on Capital Radio (his Bible of the air) or because an accident cannot be ruled out, or because it is not entirely out of the question that he, though in the rudest of health, may have a heart attack. These are the inscrutable ways of Government Car Service drivers, and it is absolutely no good questioning them, because one time in fifty you will barely be on time and then your driver will look at you in triumphant self-vindication.

Curiously, if you go by train he will not be in the least worried about getting you to the station on time. Your journey will be routine: no station manager, no reserved compartment, though at any rate a first-class reserved seat. If you fly by scheduled internal flight there will be the same lack of ceremony. Sometimes, particularly if you are on an urgent or special mission, you will be allowed to use a Royal Air Force executive jet, and this will change the pattern somewhat. You will fly from Northolt rather than Heathrow, and will be saluted off the ground by an officer of more than minor rank. Instead of the strange replica of a lunch box which British Airways offer on some of their flights there will be a tray full of canapés as at an elegant cocktail party. Very occasionally you will go by helicopter, starting from Battersea Heliport, a travel terminus operated with such lack of pomp that quite likely the official in charge (if by good fortune such a person can be found) will have no idea who you are, why you have come or where you are going. Eventually your craft will be traced and readied, and you will prepare yourself for the queasy moment when the noisy object in which you are imprisoned yaws violently as it seeks a passage through London's taller buildings (nothing, you will discover, compared to having to find the roof of one skyscraper out of hundreds in the fog of São Paulo).

However you travel, and whatever your purpose, you will be accompanied by: one Private Secretary, carrying in his anonymous government-issue brown or black leather briefcase the briefing for your trip (which he will press upon you the moment you get into the car), his Ed McBain novel and his mobile telephone to which he will appear indissolubly attached as if by prosthetic surgery; one official from the relevant policy division, carrying in his anonymous government-issue brown or black leather briefcase *his* copy of the briefing plus voluminous files to amplify this if needed, together with the collected works of Ossian which he has brought to read for pleasure; and one Press Officer, who will have brought with him nothing but a copy of the *Daily Mail*, so that you will have to take pity on him and allow him to read the full set of daily newspapers you have had brought along. These three will converse with each other about civil service matters, paying no attention to you and thus letting you get on with *your* Ed McBain. Since you are the minister you will carry nothing.

More likely than not you will be travelling to visit a factory, a shipyard, a steel mill or related establishment if you are in an industrial department, or a housing estate if you are at the Department of the Environment. Visiting a housing estate is not as simple as it sounds. It involves being met at the station by the representative of the local district council and taken to one of its many town halls (a legacy of Peter Walker's lavish and so far unexplained reform of local government) where, passing people standing at counters or windows and arguing over their council tax bills, you will arrive at the Mayor's Parlour or post-local-government-reform equivalent. Here you will meet a lot of councillors and have coffee. You will next have lunch. It will then be time to visit the housing estate, travelling in a convoy of cars more splendid than anything you have seen in Whitehall. On the estate various unoffending housewives will be waiting uneasily to receive you.

Remember that you are invading someone's home, and try to do so leaving as little upset behind you as possible. Remember, too that the someone is a voter. Make sure that the local MP (if, of course a member of your own party) is close by you for the photographs that will be taken; it is more important for his picture than yours to appear in the local newspaper. On one of these visits I kept ushering in the very new Labour MP and forcing him to shake hands with each householder, until he drew me aside and hissed: 'Gerald, we're not canvassing!' I replied, firmly, 'You're always canvassing' and made him shake hands with his constituent. I am glad to report that when some years later I visited this MP's constituency on a factory tour he had become uncontrollable, constantly breaking away to shake hands with people. Whether because of this or not, he unexpectedly held an extremely marginal seat in the 1979 election.

If you are an industrial minister and visiting a factory or similar establishment, the routine will be unvarying. Upon arrival you will be ushered into the board room for coffee (of which your Private Secretary will not partake, since he will have persuaded someone to lead him to a telephone, a terrestrial instrument with reliable reception being preferable even to his own beloved mobile phone). There will then be a presentation of what goes on at the factory, accompanied by explanatory viewgraphs; despite my best efforts I have never yet, either in Britain or abroad (where they also have them in profusion), sat through a viewgraph show without falling asleep. This is a comment upon myself rather than the quality of the entertainment. After this will come lunch. Then there will be the tour of the factory or shipyard, during which a deputed functionary of the host establishment in order to conform to a timetable will seek to hustle you along at so frenzied a pace as to make you appear to be taking part in a silent film run at the wrong speed. He will keep apologizing to you for doing this and you, running breathlessly to keep up with him, will assure him that he is doing his job as it must be done. As often as you dare you will break away to speak to a worker who, full of enthusiasm (or at any rate welcoming any opportunity to interrupt a boring routine), will explain to you exactly what he is doing; at this your escort will show signs of despair.

Then you will go to the canteen, where you will meet the shop stewards. Often you will have to insist upon this. At one factory in the North West I had to threaten to cancel my visit before the management would agree to my meeting the workers' representatives, and often such a meeting will be regarded (by others, though emphatically not by you) as an optional extra which can be omitted when time presses. When I visited one British Aerospace factory in 1978 the management (whether deliberately or not is a matter for debate) so arranged my programme that by the time I reached the place where I was to meet the shop stewards I was so late that they had got tired of waiting and gone home. I did not blame them, and returned two weeks later in order to have my discussion with them.

It is an interesting and happy fact that when you walk into the board room for the viewgraph presentation, the board of directors will rise respectfully in their places. When you enter the canteen for your meeting with shop stewards they will only continue with their conversation for one or two minutes before noticing that you have arrived.

You will be left alone with the shop stewards by management, who will return at the end of your meeting and take you back to the board room for tea, at which they may try to find out what the shop stewards said to you. At this point – or, if it suits the local press, radio and television better, somewhat earlier – you will have a press conference. Your Private Secretary may have absented himself several times to telephone the office with news of your latest indiscretion, but he will never be absent from your press conference, because here your opportunities for misbehaviour will be at their zenith. When visiting a paper-mill at Bury, I was responsible for the almost total demoralization of the conscientious Private Secretary who accompanied me since, at a press conference in this paper-making constituency where the Labour Member of Parliament was defending a majority of 442, I insisted on announcing a government scheme of assistance to the paper industry when it had not yet been quite approved by the appropriate Cabinet Committee. Scarcely were the words out of my lips than the Private Secretary had darted out of the room, and seconds later defensive briefing was being prepared in the department's press office. Happily, the scheme was speedily endorsed, and the MP was subsequently re-elected.

Not all of your industrial visits will be for routine purposes. At the Department of Industry I had responsibility for the Post Office, and carried out the traditional Postmaster-General's visit to see the Christmas post being sorted; I did it in Manchester, partly in my own constituency. During the passage of the Aircraft and Ship-building Industries Bill I visited nearly every aircraft factory and shipyard in the country to discuss industrial democracy with the shop stewards, in fulfilment of an undertaking I had given at committee stage. You will also address conferences and study courses, and open exhibitions. Be careful that you have your script with you, not only for your Private Secretary's peace of mind but also for your own. At the opening of an exhibition at the Design Centre I was certain that I could deliver the short speech that was needed without notes, and therefore cast my script aside. In the middle of my remarks I suddenly forgot what I was supposed to say next, and no words of any kind on any subject would come into my head. A pause ensued, of to me mammoth dimensions, before I could think of anything at all to say, and I was never again so over-confident as to believe that I could do without at least some notes to buttress me.

Sometimes you will be sent out on a special mission. From the Department of the Environment I was dispatched to travel around the country addressing special regional conferences at which I urged representatives of local authorities to increase their building programmes; I was later denounced by the Opposition spokesman for irresponsibly stirring up councils to build more houses. During my brief period at the Cabinet Office I visited Regional Emergency Committees set up to cope with the consequences of the 1979 winter strikes, and found that they had been getting on perfectly well without me. Again at DoE I went by helicopter to Flixborough, in Lincolnshire, where there had been a ghastly factory disaster of massive dimensions, to see what help the government could provide. It was an eerie and disquieting experience to fly through a cloudless June sky and then suddenly hover above a scene of devastation. Once again, though they naturally welcomed government assistance, the local people were coping with great resource.

Your travels within Britain may be routine or urgent. Your travels abroad will be ceremonial. If you are a minister of any but the highest rank, you have to leave your own country to become Someone. Your driver will call at your home to take you to the airport so early that you could easily be there in time to travel standby. Arriving at Heathrow you will not be required to huddle with the crowds at the departure terminal, but will instead be driven straight to a VIP lounge named after some prominent aviator of the past. There you will be offered coffee and biscuits while your Private Secretary hands over to an omni-competent janissary your passports and tickets (before secreting himself in a corner to make a last-minute telephone call to the office). Your government car, in a last despairing attempt to claim you for its own, will then take you out to the aircraft, which the other passengers will all have already boarded.

You will of course be flying first class, provided the line and route possess such a facility. You will also, if at all possible, be flying on a British airline. Until privatisation the government's airline of choice was British Airways, a sensible requirement since BA at its best provides a crisp and courteous service no other airline can rival. Such service is especially important on flights lasting very many hours, which can turn into nightmares coupled with insomnia. This is not to say that other airlines do not have their points. The moment you got aboard a plane belonging to Air Nepal, to pluck an example at random, beautiful, robed Hindu ladies instantly plied you with hard liquor, Air Nepal not being a member of the International Air Transport Association and accordingly not bound by its killjoy restrictive rules.

When you arrive at your overseas destination you will be met at the landing steps of your plane by an official from the host government there to welcome you, and by either the British Ambassador or High Commissioner or at any rate some relatively senior member of the embassy staff (whom your Private Secretary will at once draw aside in order to make arrangements for an immediate telephone call to the office in London as his very first action upon arrival at the Residence or Governor's Palace where you will be staying). You are put up at these frequently luxurious establishments for two reasons: first, because it saves money; second, because it keeps you out of mischief and/or spares you embarrassment of the kind to which I was subjected when I visited Singapore to join Concorde for a dauntingly named 'endurance' flight to Melbourne.

On this occasion I stayed at a bizarre Holiday Inn which, for reasons that no doubt seemed good to its proprietors, was under the delusion that it was situated in the Alps. Through its grotesquely decorated lobby wandered pretty Chinese waitresses disconcertingly garbed in dirndls. I arrived very late and had to get up very early. I went straight to bed and soon fell asleep, but before long was wakened by the ringing of the telephone. Groggy with fatigue I heard through the earpiece the voice of someone who seemed to have learned English by watching films of Peter Lorre playing Mr Moto, and who solicitously asked me if he could provide me with comforting female companionship. I responded with epithets which would have done credit to George Sanders at his most crushing, slammed down the telephone and tried to get back to sleep. Next day I dutifully reported the incident to the High Commissioner. My Private Secretary, who was made of considerably sterner stuff than the one who had been upset by my paper-making exploit, complained that the telephone call should have been routed through to him, since all such approaches should be made through the Private Secretary.

None of this of course would have happened had I stayed at the High Commissioner's Residence. There, on my arrival, my luggage would have been unpacked by a deeply courteous member of the household staff, who would have seized every garment he could lay his hands on to launder or dry-clean, or at least to press. My breakfast would have been brought to my room, and my day mapped out by various aides assigned to me by the High Commission (thus leaving my Private Secretary free to telephone).

Staying with the Ambassador, High Commissioner or Consul-General will give you the opportunity to see how British diplomats live abroad. Some of them do startlingly well for themselves, with grand houses and armies of servants. Others live very modestly. All will have their basic needs provided for by the Overseas Estate Department, who will supply the furniture you sit on and the crockery you eat from.

You will also have the chance to judge their quality, and here too the differences will be wide. Some will be excellent representatives of their country, brisk and businesslike, yet full of humour and diplomatically very skilled. Of Ambassadors in post when I visited the capitals where they were located, Michael Wilford (Tokyo), Anthony Parsons (Tehran), Derek Dodson (Brasilia), and Peter Ramsbotham (Washington) struck me as exceptional; I did not go to Washington when Peter Jay was there, but from meetings at which I briefed him in Britain I judged that he was of comparable quality. Others were less good, and some were dreadful, representatives of a Britain unknown to most of its citizens and clearly out of sympathy with the Labour government they were there to represent. One British High Commissioner demonstrated this in an

unusual way. He was sitting with his wife by the swimming-pool –
another frequent ambassadorial perquisite – at his Residence when
I went out to join them for tea. I noticed lying on the grass by his
side a huge motor horn and asked what its purpose might be. 'Oh,'
he said, 'we blow it to call the servants. Would you like a go?' I
decidedly did not want a go, since I had no wish to cause alarmed
servants to come running for no reason at the sound of this mon-
strous instrument. Trying ineffectively to be flippant, I replied, 'I
don't think I'm a member of the right union.' Her Majesty's representative crushed me with the retort, 'That's a very Labour reply,'
and turned his attention to the cucumber sandwiches.

At least, however, he did provide food. On one occasion when I
stayed at the official British residence in Paris, our Ambassador
went out to dinner without making any provision for feeding my
civil servants and myself. Returning hungry very late from an
engagement we ransacked the Residence but could find nothing in
the kitchen, and not even my Private Secretary's most valiant efforts
on the telephone could locate any member of the household who
might be able to help. In the end he went out for sandwiches. The
Ambassador's wife was most concerned when she heard about this
on her return, and after a prolonged search unearthed some Ryvita
which she hospitably handed over to us.

Another of our diplomatic representatives – and an excellent one
too – regarded food as less important than drink. I first noticed
this at 8.30 one morning when he came to fetch me for our day's
engagements and he breathed on me when we were enclosed
together in a very small lift. Thereafter he would vanish from time
to time for prolonged periods, returning in a much improved mood
with such information as that he had had to go and buy a railway
platform ticket. Another would have benefited from such a self-
indulgent regimen, since he forced me to climb a mountain immediately upon my arrival following an all-night flight. Yet another
Ambassador – and again a very good one – spoke . . . quite . . .
extraordinarily . . . slowly, which made for some tension while one
awaited the conclusion of his remarks. He stayed up until the early
hours conversing with an official I had brought with me, clever and
agreeable but with a tendency to reminisce at length. At around 2
a.m. my official ventured self-deprecatingly to remark: 'I suppose

I'm boring you,' to which the Ambassador responded, 'You . . . could . . . say . . . that.'

There will be many reasons why you need to travel abroad. These will include visits to compare foreign industries with our own (steel-mills in Korea and Japan, paper-mills in Sweden) or to examine industries you hope to foster in Britain (Smart Valley, California). You may visit the Paris or Berlin air shows or the Poseidon shipping exhibition in Athens where, believe it or not, your tour of the British stands will boost morale. You may go to inspect works for which your department is responsible, a motive which took me on the unlikely journey from the Department of the Environment to Katmandu. At first I could not believe that there was any valid reason for me to go there, but a civil servant at Permanent Secretary level came to persuade me. The Property Services Agency were responsible for building a stretch of inter-nationally sponsored road in southern Nepal as part of an aid project, and they wanted a minister to go and see it, by his presence emphasizing Britain's commitment to helping Nepal and at the same time confirming that the road was fit for Prince Charles to inspect on a forthcoming visit.

Whether Prince Charles ever got there I do not know but I did, in a tiny plane racketing precariously through the monsoon. I stayed overnight in an encampment, lodged in a hut of the kind that Jungle Jim used to inhabit in the comics I read when safe at home in Leeds, visited the staff club, which was a replica of the setting in the first act of Puccini's *Girl of the Golden West*, and went out to see the road, which was throughout very muddy and at one point blocked by a kind of landslide. This was certainly doing my duty after the pleasures of Bangkok, which I had visited en route on business too complicated to recount, and where I had caught diarrhoea. Katmandu itself was lovely, but almost as muddy as the road.

You will travel abroad to attend international conferences, and to take part in discussions and negotiations with ministers from other countries. Occasionally you will get an assignment which makes a visit to a road in Nepal seem quite routine: such as, for example, representing your country at the government hearing in Wash-ington to decide whether Concorde should be allowed to land in the United States. If you are involved in a project like Concorde it will dog you throughout your ministerial career. I went on that endurance flight. I had to visit Paris for repeated negotiations with the French about this extraordinary aircraft's finances and future. I toured the factories in Toulouse and Bristol where the plane was built, in Bristol receiving from the workers on a huge poster the encouraging promise: PLEASE EXTEND THE CONCORDE LINE AND YOU WILL BE OUR VALENTINE. I travelled from Paris to Rio and back by Concorde, and was airsick at a height greater than had been attained by anyone except astronauts. And I went to Washington.

After I was asked to take on the job I only gradually realized that what was expected from me was not a quiet chat with an American fellow minister but a histrionic public appearance at a hearing which was also a media event. Nor was I prepared for the indoctrination I was made to undergo, with a rehearsal of the event staged in the Washington Embassy Rotunda by Ken Binning, the fiendish civil servant then in charge of the Concorde project. One of our legal advisers was a former Assistant Attorney-General of the United States who had been got rid of by President Nixon, no doubt because he was afraid of him. I certainly was, as this forbidding figure impersonating the Secretary for Transportation cross-examined me without mercy while I haltingly proffered my evidence. The rehearsal went on for hours, and was so numbing in its effect that the actual hearing before the admirable Secretary Coleman was painless, his interruptions seeming mere pinpricks after what I had already been made to undergo.

It was a pretty weird day altogether. We took our lunch across the road from the Department of Transportation in the Smithsonian Institution, where souvenirs of the revolution were being prepared for the United States bicentenary. I stayed at the hearing for the whole of the proceedings, and was there when a representative of one local community near Kennedy Airport went to the rostrum to give evidence against Concorde. Like many who lived in that district she was Jewish, and while she waited a couple of seats away from me I was tempted to say to her, 'What's a nice Jewish girl like you doing in a place like this?' But I thought she might take it amiss, so I refrained. We won, and I was able to travel both to Washington and New York on the inaugural Concorde flights.

Wherever you travel, and for whatever purpose, there will be certain set events on your every visit. Your Ambassador will give a dinner for you, at which you will eat precisely the food you would have at an official dinner in Lancaster House or Downing Street, right down to the brown consommé which I am certain is kept in a huge vat beneath the Cabinet Office. Your foreign hosts will give a dinner or lunch for you. You will give a press conference, and possibly appear on radio or television. If you are involved in a delicate negotiation this will be most important, since it is necessary that your fellow countrymen know you have been fighting abroad for Britain; your own government will learn about it because the Ambassador will send the Foreign Office a telegram reporting on the success or otherwise of your visit. You yourself will write your own report on your return. But you will really know whether you have succeeded when the Hawk trainers are sold to Finland or the BAC I-II deal is signed with Romania – or Concorde lands in New York.

As you travel back to Britain you will remember such people as the member of your audience at the lecture you gave to the English-Speaking Union in St Louis, who asked you with the utmost seriousness to tell him about the socialist policies Mrs Thatcher intended to introduce into Britain. You will recall the food you could not keep down in Pusan, Korea, and – also in Korea – your efforts, not entirely successful, to fend off explorations of your person by the kimonoed hostess solicitously placed next to you at an official government dinner. And then your plane will land at Heathrow; you will see your driver's face grinning out of the car waiting for you on the tarmac and when you arrive at the VIP lounge your Private Secretary will rush off to telephone the office. You are home, and perhaps you have not done too much damage. Maybe you have even helped a little.

16

How to be Communautaire

You may love it, you may loathe it, but you have to accept it. Britain is a member of the European Union. The structure of the Union is quite simple, once you get the hang of it. There is the Parliament, elected by voters in the member countries, whose most sweeping powers are to throw out the Budget (which it did late in 1979) and throw out the Commission (so far left undisturbed). The Commission is superficially the Union's Secretariat. The Commissioners, however, are very much more than civil servants. They are the people who run the Union full time. They are not elected, but nominated by member governments, a maximum of two per country. Breathtakingly well paid, they sit in palatial offices (which make the man who ran up a little something for Reginald Freeson's predecessor – remember? if not, see page 12 – look like an under-achiever) right at the top of the Commission's headquarters building in the heart of Brussels. They have vast numbers of functionaries working for them turning out tons – sorry, tonnes – of documents in numerous languages. Unless and until the Parliament throws them out, they are responsible to no one, not even the government that nominated them. And yet they make regulations or directives which are laws, overriding the statutes of member countries. Personally they can be nice or nasty, competent or unable to cope, but they are immensely powerful.

Many of the powers the Commissioners wield stem from decisions made by the Ministerial Council meetings. It is at this stage, rather than through the Parliament, that any democratic control of the Union is exercised. The ministers act as authorized or instructed by their governments, but their actions are subject to the wishes of their domestic Parliaments, even though the Parliaments themselves are subject to the Treaties which, in turn, the Parliaments themselves have ratified. In Britain this ratification was accomplished through the European Communities Act of 1972, a statute in which Britain – according to the way you look at it – voted away her Parliament's sovereignty to a gang of irresponsible bureaucrats or else voluntarily surrendered her selfish national interests in order to help achieve the ideals of greater internationalism.

How much contact you have with this elaborate structure will greatly depend on your department. Many departments have relatively little to do with the Union. Others – the Foreign Office, naturally enough, the Treasury, the Ministry of Agriculture, the Department of Trade and Industry – are constantly entangled with them. Certain other departments are sporadically involved; these include the Overseas Development Administration (intimately concerned with the mysteries surrounding the Lome Covention).

Your contacts with the Union can be at several levels. You may have meetings with Commissioners, at their request or at yours. You may have meetings with fellow ministers from Union countries bilaterally or multilaterally, but outside the formal machinery of the Union. You will be required to attend Ministerial Council meetings.

You will meet Commissioners because, for one or other of you, such a meeting is the only way of solving a problem. If they really need to meet you they will even brave the cross-Channel airways system (no mean challenge, as we shall see) to attend upon you in your office in London. If they do this, they will be late. This will be because the Commissioner, having decided, a little like Nero Wolfe venturing reluctantly forth from his brownstone house in New York, upon this daunting safari, will want to fit in as much as possible. He will therefore visit several ministers, arriving progressively later for each one on his schedule. Finally he will arrive in your office amid a flourish of bureaucrats. These will come from his Cabinet and his Services. We may pause at this point to note that the European Union has a language of its own, a language which without prejudice we shall call Eurojargon. In Eurojargon, a Commissioner's Private Office is his Cabinet and his civil servants, or officials, are his Services. This is as good a moment as any to draw attention to such other standard items of Eurojargon as 'envelope' and 'margins'. An envelope is a limit within which budgetary dispositions can be juggled; having learned its meaning you can forget it, since it will not recur in this narrative. Margins are areas, physical as well as metaphysical, where informal contacts can be conducted during Council meetings; these, alas, we shall encounter again.

The Commissioner's Cabinet representative will be a burly, beautifully dressed young man who will take notes incessantly, in blatant rivalry with your own Private Secretary who, on his mettle, will feverishly be doing the same thing. The men from his Services will be like minor Shakespearean characters (indeed in my office two of them were always known as Rosencrantz and Guildenstern) who will be in a state of needless terror that at any moment their Commissioner is going to make unwarranted concessions. Unless, of course, you are about to take him out to lunch – Commissioners being willing guests and even more willing hosts – the Commissioner will be in a hurry, either to get on to his appointment with the next minister, or to dash out to Heathrow there to emplane for the blessed security of Brussels.

It may well be, though, that it is you who will be going to see the Commissioner in Brussels. You will, however, be spared the tribulation of having to see him in Luxembourg. The European Communities, as they then were, used to have two headquarters, mainly because Luxembourg would not tolerate being left out of things. So twice a year the Commissioners, the Cabinets, the Services and the tonnes of documents were all transported bodily to this pretty little city which, as one of my Private Secretaries once feelingly put it, closes down promptly, at nine o'clock every night. You could not go to Luxembourg and back in a day as you can to Brussels, but had to stay overnight and book into an hotel, the place being not only almost inaccessible but chronically fogbound. You needed to be careful which hotel to choose; there was one called the Grand Hotel Cravat which was certainly an hotel but was equally certainly not grand; and I never saw a cravat there.

You will have to go to Brussels to see the Commissioner because you will be desperate to settle a problem urgently. The Services, who will have been in discussion with your officials, will have been intransigent. You will have tried to speak to the Commissioner on the telephone, but he will have been unavailable. So one day you will get on an aeroplane and go to see him. You will, at any rate, no longer have to fly on a half-aeroplane. If the timing of your meeting is such that you cannot avoid it, you will have to disregard the ruling to use a British airline and fly Sabena; and there was a time when the Sabena fleet used to include certain aircraft which came to a sudden stop halfway along. You got on, walked through the cabin, and instead of arriving eventually at the partition that separated you from the pilot on his flight deck, you came to a blank wall. Behind this blank wall was a huge cargo compartment, inserted to increase the revenues of the thrifty Belgians; beyond this lay the flight deck.

With you will be your Private Secretary, an official from the relevant policy division of your department, and your department's specially designated EU official. During most of my time at the Department of Industry this post was held by a superb lady who after years of baleful experience was wise to the ways of the Common Market and could anticipate every move its denizens would make; the only dubious advice I ever knew her give was to stay at the Grand Hotel Cravat. You will in any case need three civil servants with you because the briefs that your party will be carrying will be monumental in volume. When you arrive in Brussels you will be met by an official from the United Kingdom Embassy to the Union whose doomed existence, like a bureaucratic version of the Flying Dutchman, is to travel back and forth between Brussels and its airport welcoming and seeing off itinerant ministers.

Waiting outside the airport will be a car, driven by a hardened British driver, which will weave its way through the suburbs of Brussels – always a fillip for those nostalgic for Stoke-on-Trent on a wet Sunday afternoon – to the British Mission's headquarters. And there, unless he is too busy to see you, will be the British Ambassador to the Communities. During my period at the Department of Industry the holder of this post was Sir Donald Maitland, a man for whom it would be difficult for me to express or even exaggerate my respect and admiration. A small, dour Scotsman, and a career diplomat who had also been Edward Heath's Press Officer at Number Ten, Sir Donald was, quite simply, brilliant. He knew and understood everything that was going on, anticipated every devious move made by the Commission and member countries, toiled like a Japanese car worker, was totally without illusions, was utterly loyal to his government and, if the qualities of this paragon were not sufficient already, had a sense of humour which can only be described as pawky.

The Ambassador will brief you (in the absence of your Private

Secretary who will have gone to telephone, but from now on we will take that for granted) and you will then go across to the Breydel building to see the Commissioner, riding up in a lift to a waiting area several times the floor space of your entire department. There will be idiosyncratic magazines for you to read while you wait, such as the *Fire Brigades Journal*. Then you will be ushered into an office with a commanding view of the office blocks of Brussels and there waiting for you will be the Commissioner, the burly, beautifully dressed young man to take notes, and Rosencrantz and Guildenstern or their confrères. You will be offered cold coffee out of tiny cups, and the meeting will begin.

Whether you meet him in London or Brussels, your encounters with the Commissioner will follow an identical routine. He will outline to you his predicament, paint dramatically a picture of the pressure the other Commissioners are putting on him because of his culpable weakness due to his personal fondness for you, and then in the kindest possible way make a series of unacceptable demands. You will respond by pledging your eternal fidelity to the spirit of the EU (this is known as being Communautaire) before going on to add that your Parliament will not accept anything the Commissioner has demanded and in your turn making a series of demands at which the Commissioner will dramatically flinch as he listens. You will then get down to business. Every time the Commissioner makes a concession, which he will have planned in advance, his Services will blench, possibly even tugging at his coat sleeve. Every time you respond your undisciplined officials will smirk.

To such a meeting there are two possible outcomes. One is agreement; another, much more likely, is for your officials and the Commissioner's Services to arrange a further meeting, at which they will seek to prepare a formula for the Commissioner and yourself to discuss at a later date to be decided. The meeting will conclude in one of two ways: either you will dash off to the airport to get a plane back to London; or, if timing makes this impossible, you will be taken out to an inedibly lavish lunch by the official from the British Mission who has been assigned to keep an eye on you. There, in one of Brussels' many gourmet restaurants, you will try to decide who has managed to steal a march upon whom, concluding gloomily that probably the Commissioner had the upper hand.

Meetings with fellow ministers from the Union will be less

formal. You will confer in their office in their capital or in your department in London. You will meet as fellow politicians with Parliaments and electorates to account to and, within the policy guidelines set to each of you by your Cabinet, you will try to be flexible. Either you will try to trade off concessions in order to reach an agreement – 'You withdraw your block on what we want, and we shall do the same for you' – or else you will be confederates trying to work out a common plan of action to win over an unreliable or indecisive Ministerial Council. And it will be at the Council of Ministers that the issue will be decided. Some votes will be rendered vital by the unanimity rule by which the most important decisions are still generally made. In other words, each of you has a veto and is perfectly ready to exercise it.

Although there are other Ministerial Councils – for example, the Research Council – the principal Council at which Community business is done is the Foreign Ministers' Council, held approximately monthly. Generally this will be attended for your country by a Minister of State from the Foreign and Commonwealth Office; but other departments will be represented by ministers when one of their areas of policy is being discussed. If that means you, you will enter a large room dominated by a vast oblong table. Scattered around the table will be microphones, carafes and glasses. Behind the table and concentric with it will be further tables. This is where your advisers will sit. Behind glass panels lurk the interpreters, for this is government by headphone. You, together with your Ambassador and perhaps a fellow minister, will sit in the places at the main table marked out for your country. There will be places for every member country, together with the President (who holds office for six months before another country has its turn to take over all the Council Presidencies) and the Commission.

Considerably later than the time the meeting is due to begin (Eurojargon being matched by Eurotime), the President will call everyone to order. He may then, somewhat to the participants' surprise, start on the announced business. More likely there will be news of a change in the agenda, and a certain amount of procedural haggling. Eventually the meeting proper will get underway, everyone except a minority of complacently exhibitionist multi-linguists having donned headphones and tuned to the channel that translates into their language (there being, unfortunately, no music channel). The President will announce that, upon whatever vexed topic the Council has met to resolve, he will begin with a Tour de Table. This translated from Eurojargon means that he is going to go round the table so that every delegation in turn can say what it thinks.

If this is what every delegation actually does, he will be a very lucky President. What is much more likely is that the representatives of the smaller countries, who believe passionately in the Union, will fretfully demand that the four largest powers – France, Germany, Italy and the United Kingdom – be less self-regarding and more Communautaire. Next, each of the representatives of the four largest powers will pledge himself to be Communautaire and then use the Eurojargon for, 'I pass.' They are all waiting to see what will happen. They are also hoping that, if they have instructions to be difficult, some other country will be difficult first, so that they can avoid as much as possible the obloquy that Denmark and Belgium are perfectly ready to heap upon them. The countries most likely to be troublesome are Italy and France. Italy will be troublesome at length, while everyone else (especially any countries that are delighted that Italy is being troublesome on their behalf) will exchange sighs of fatigue and reproof. France may be troublesome quite briefly, but when France is troublesome France is really troublesome. A French representative can sit for several hours at a time simply repeating his instructions; I personally think they are marvellous at it, especially since when they are on your side they are absolutely indomitable allies.

After the Tour de Table the Commissioner will intervene, pleading for consensus and warning of catastrophe if agreement is not reached. After this the horse-trading will begin. Fixed positions will begin to fray around the edges. Maybe there will indeed be agreement. But maybe there will not; and then you will know that you are in for a very long session. There will be one sure sign of this. From time to time attendants, looking like Donald Sinden but Belgian, will bring round trays of coffee. If these attendants suddenly begin carrying round glasses of whisky instead, you will know that the bush telegraph has circulated the news that there is to be a late sitting. Various things can then happen. The President can order an adjournment so that there can be discussions in the margins. This means that various ministers will go out into the corridor and have a row. Or he can order an adjournment for dinner. This is Eurojargon for huge pieces of French bread with ham or cheese, and glasses of wine. Or he can order a restricted session, which means that, except for the one who draws the short straw and has to remain, your advisers can escape to go out for a decent dinner.

If the negotiations in the margins are not successful the discussion in the Council Chamber can go on for many hours, indeed all night. Tempers fray, the Commissioners become more desperate, the Italians more voluble, the French more inflexible. Quite possibly you will reach agreement. This will depend on the instructions under which you and your fellow ministers are operating. If it is you who are having to be difficult, it will suit you best if you have been sent to Brussels with an unalterable Cabinet instruction. Otherwise your Ambassador will be desperately pressing you to make concessions since he knows that, if the Ministerial Council fails to agree, the subject will be thrown to one of the regular meetings of Permanent Representatives (COREPER in Eurojargon) and this topic will be added to his already unmanageable overload of work. Eventually, having agreed or failed to agree, you will all stagger out into the Belgian night and towards whichever of the many intolerable hotels in Brussels you have been consigned.

It may well be, of course, that you yourself have been the President in charge of the meeting. I held such a presidency, of the Research Council, for six months, the Permanent Secretary of my department having come to see me and ruthlessly flattered me into agreeing to accept this unenviable assignment. During my presidency the dominating issue was the location of an atomic venture called JET, the Joint European Torus. Our Cabinet had decided it wanted this to be at Culham in Oxfordshire and it was the job of Tony Benn, as Energy Secretary, to get it. The Prime Minister himself had been involved in the discussions (none of them in the margins), and we thought we had the whole thing sewn up. However, shortly after the Council began, it became clear that a deal we thought we had made with Germany by which JET would come to Culham had become unstuck. The German minister had come to see me in my President's room before the Council meeting to confirm that, in the light of our previous talks, he would accept the verdict of the Council.

Unfortunately, as soon as the meeting began it became clear that undertakings had been abandoned which we thought were firmly agreed. The meeting began to go badly against location at Culham. The only outcome that could save Britain was a failure to come to a decision. And as the meeting went on the unfortunate view of the Germans was that the President was preventing a decision. Other representatives, on the other hand, were perfectly content with the way the meeting was being conducted, none more so than the French, who were seeking to prevent agreement on this matter for some arcane purpose of their own. They had the splendid advantage of not even being represented by a minister but only by an official, who had no power whatever to make concessions of any kind. The meeting, which before it began I had complacently vowed would not go on beyond 10 p.m., lasted until dawn, when the German representative left furiously thwarted, others just went away tired, the Frenchman was perfectly fresh and ready to continue indefinitely, and Britain lived to fight another day. In the end, though many months afterwards, JET went to Culham.

If you hold an EU presidency, you should fulfil the responsibility with the seriousness it merits. Curiously, the Union does not provide its Council Presidents with any staff. All those bureaucrats are there for the Commissioners, not for you; the staff at your department will have to suffice. However, you will be welcome in your presidential capacity at any Union facilities for which your Council is responsible. For the Research Council this meant the EEC's main Research Centre at Ispra near Como, Italy. After the indecisive meeting on JET, I decided to go to Ispra in order to assure the staff there that their Budget would eventually be approved so that they would be able to proceed with their activities. Following my invariable practice I had a meeting with the trade union representatives, who on this occasion did not offer me a Valentine. Instead I was given a tour of the facilities and received the impression that all the mad inventors from the whole of Western Europe had gathered together in one rain-sodden spot to experiment with solar energy, laser beams and other matters too abstruse for me to comprehend. I was, in addition, taken to a concert at La Scala, Milan, making the forty-minute journey from Ispra door to door in eighteen minutes thanks to the selfless if murderous devotion of the plain-clothes detectives who had been assigned to protect me (whether from the research workers or the Red Brigade was not made absolutely clear).

From all the meetings you attend on Union business you are likely to take away with you the impression of a massive, well-oiled machine going nowhere. Those who oppose British membership will nod their heads sagely and say they expected nothing else. Those, however, who have reposed great hopes in the EU will be sad to witness their noble ideal smothered in paper and bureaucracy, with the bigger powers plunging through the maze in search of national self-interest while the smaller countries desperately try to persuade them of the importance of being Communautaire.

17

How to Get On with the Press

Harold Wilson said of Frank Cousins, when he was Minister of Technology, that his achievements as a minister were in inverse ratio to his press coverage. Cousins, in other words, was a good minister but nobody knew about it. If you turn out to be a good minister, make sure everyone knows about it. Only the press, television and radio can tell them: there is no message without the media.

You will meet the press wherever you go: in the House of Commons, in your department, when you travel. Learn to know them, and try to make the most of what they can do for you. As a minister, you are news. The most junior minister will get a packed house when he calls a press conference at his department. A leading Opposition spokesman is lucky to get enough journalists along for a meaningful game of ludo.

It is of course necessary for you to understand how the press operate. The first time that I as a journalist on the *New Statesman* interviewed Harold Wilson at Number Ten, he said to me casually: 'Your deadline's Tuesday, isn't it?' It really is useful to know things like this. No use telephoning a Sunday paper on Monday; its news desk will be closed. No use telephoning a Sunday paper on Saturday evening; most of its pages will have gone to press. Evening newspapers have to be contacted very early in the day. You should plan the timing of your press releases depending on whether you want them to have a chance of being featured in the BBC television and ITN news bulletins between 5.40 and 6 p.m., or are ready to wait for the longer bulletins at 9 and 10 p.m. Make sure that you are not putting out a good story on a day another minister has the same idea. Otherwise you will upstage each other. Make absolutely certain that you are not putting out a good story on a day when the Prime Minister is making a major pronouncement; either he will win all the headlines or else he will be very annoyed. There is inter-departmental co-ordinating machinery to prevent such clashes; but always take extra precautions yourself. Save some of your stories for parliamentary recesses. The newspapers are always short of material then, and you may well get a better show.

Parliament, though, will be the focus of your activities. As an experienced MP you will be familiar with the rather complicated system in which the press operates at Westminster. First there are the gallery reporters. They work for the 'serious' newspapers and have the assignment of reporting parliamentary debates without elaboration. As a minister you should do well out of them; though these days not much of what they are employed to report actually gets printed, objective reporting of parliamentary proceedings now being regarded as a bore. Next come the sketch writers. They treat Parliament like a theatre and write reviews of the debates. They are very selective and very capricious. Some of them are brilliant. If any of them takes a fancy to you, you will be in luck. One of them always wrote about me with high approval, and I thought him marvellous. Another was not really malevolent, but persisted in describing me as 'small'; I did not like him half so much. If you speak well in debate you may have a chance with them, but do not rely on it. One snappy response to a supplementary question can get you more coverage from the sketch writers than a major speech over which you have slaved for days. Unlike Anthony Crosland, they love frivolity.

The real political specialists at Westminster are the Lobby Correspondents. They are the journalists whose bylines have added to them such descriptions as Political Editor, Political Corres-pondent, Political Staff, Lobby Correspondent, Lobby Staff. It is they who are allowed into the Members' Lobby, which adjoins the entrance to the Commons Chamber, by the Serjeant-at-Arms. There they have the right to swoop upon you and question you. They are not allowed to sit down on the benches in the Lobby and in theory they are not allowed to take notes there, though many sensibly ignore this rule. Anything you say to them in the Lobby is off the record and cannot be attributed to you, unless you give them express permission. These journalists also have the freedom of the Ways and Means Corridor, to which they are in any case evicted from the Lobby when a Division takes place. You may in addition encounter them in the Strangers' Bar and in Annie's Bar, the latter being a small drinking place sited conspiratorially at the end of a labyrinth of corridors through which only a truly dedicated drinker (or gossip-monger) could find his way; only MPs, officers of the House and certain journalists are admitted to Annie's Bar. Your conversations with them in all these places are privileged. If you do not wish to have conversations with them then keep away from these locations, where you are fair game. Some ministers always enter the Chamber not through the Members' Lobby but from behind the Speaker's Chair. Either they are afraid that Lobby journalists will pester them or else they are unusually modest.

There are two other places where you may encounter Lobby journalists (unless, of course, they take you out to lunch, which is always worth accepting since they frequent extremely luxurious places). The first is in the Press Gallery premises, which contain a bar, a dining room and a cafeteria; but if you go up there without being invited by a journalist it will cause great resentment. The second is in the Lobby Room, located in a small cubby-hole up a winding staircase off the Upper Committee Corridor. Not all the journalists permitted into the Members' Lobby are allowed here, only those among them who are members of The Lobby, an extremely secret organization that everyone at Westminster knows about. These journalists have their own bureaucratic structure, including special rules and annually elected officers, and receive regular daily briefings from Downing Street together with briefings on Thursday afternoons from the Leader of the House. Anyone who comes into the Lobby Room does so by invitation only, and you will have to be very important and to have done something extremely newsworthy to be asked there.

The Lobby journalists are always on the look out for exclusive news, and of course you are particularly well placed to supply it. You as a minister will be involved in all sorts of portentous and confidential activities yourself; you will see very many classified documents; and you will hear fascinating gossip from government colleagues and from officials. However, be careful. First, you have signed the Official Secrets Act. Second, Prime Ministers absolutely detest leaks. Whenever they see one they begin to wonder who was the perpetrator. Sometimes it is pretty easy to tell. During one major controversy that blew up in the period of office of the Labour government of 1974–9 the newspapers suddenly all printed inside stories giving the viewpoint of one of the ministers involved. The minister himself was responsible, having invited the Lobby Correspondents of each of the major newspapers one after another to his room in the House of Commons and told them how he was feeling about things. He might well have echoed the memorable words of the movie star Lina Lamont in *Singin' in the Rain*: 'I gave an exclusive story to every paper in town.'

Sometimes, though, the origin of the exclusive story can be more mysterious. Late in 1977 James Callaghan asked me to do some work for him on the steel industry and, as was natural, this resulted in the compilation of some documents which I forwarded to him. I therefore had quite a shock over my cornflakes when one morning at breakfast I opened my *Daily Mirror* – to which as a former member of the staff I had remained a sentimentally loyal subscriber – to see the headline: '100 pages of dynamite'. Below this was an extraordinary and inaccurate travesty of what was in my documents. The article was written by Geoffrey Goodman, not only one of the – rightly – most respected journalists in Fleet Street but also an old friend of mine. I could only judge that his source was, to him, so reliable that he had felt no need to check with me. I later discovered that his source could not in theory have been more reliable. It was someone who worked at Number Ten, not a member of the Prime Minister's own staff, clearly acting entirely without the Prime Minister's knowledge, and motivated by what was to me inexplicable malice. After that incident I became quite as averse to leaks as the most leak-conscious Prime Minister.

This article was so hostile to me that I at any rate was clearly absolved from responsibility for it. Prime Ministers do, though, like to find out who is responsible for leaks and even have, for the most heinous cases, a leaks procedure to track down careless talkers. Soon after she became Prime Minister Margaret Thatcher found that some of her government's private documents were vulnerable to leaks, and she swiftly became as keen a leak-hunter as any of her predecessors. The only real solution to the problem is one that Lee Howard, an excellent editor of the *Daily Mirror*, asked me to pass on to Harold Wilson during a period of unease between the Prime Minister and the Press. 'Please tell Harold', Lee said to me, 'to stop reading the newspapers.' I did, but he did not. And you will not either. Every morning one of your first actions on arriving at your department will be to study the photostat sheaf of press cuttings that your Private Secretary will bring in to you. You will be disappointed if it does not contain something about you, and upset if what is said about you is not favourable.

Second only to Westminster your department is the place where you will most frequently meet the press. You will hold press conferences here, not only for Lobby journalists who will come across from the House of Commons, but for specialist journalists too. There is, for example, a corps of industrial journalists almost as tightly organized as the Lobby reporters. There are also aviation journalists, energy journalists, planning journalists and all kinds of other experts who will wish to write about you. It is useful to meet regularly those interested in your department and to keep them posted about your activities. You will from time to time call press conferences when you publish a Bill or take some other political initiative. Everyone will have their own approach, but I recommend two rules. First, always speak on the record. If you do this there can be no doubt about what you have said, and no danger of leaks. Second, speak to the writing journalists before you give your radio and television interviews. There is always a Pied Piper enticement for a politician at the prospect of a television appearance. But remember that while you reach many more people on television it is the comments of the writing journalists which make or destroy a reputation. Further, what is written in newspapers or magazines lives on in archives (whether computerized, microfilmed or even old-fashioned cuttings), to be repeated by other writers for years to come.

Your department's huge information division will set up your press conference. You will have sitting by you not only a Press Officer but also senior civil servants from the relevant policy division. If you are asked a question and do not know the answer, always say so and either pass the question to an official who does know or else arrange for the Press Officer to supply the information later. The journalists are aware that you are not omniscient, and will accept a confession of ignorance. If you attempt to stumble along rather than make the confession, they will be scornful. At the television and radio interviews afterwards, one of the Press Officers (together with your Private Secretary) will always be present, for what purpose is not clear; at any rate, I never knew either one of them to interrupt the proceedings, smash the camera, stop the tape recorder or otherwise emphasize his presence. In your interview do not be distracted by such irrelevancies as the questions that the TV person will put to you. Decide in advance exactly what information you wish to communicate to the viewer at home, and make sure you say it whatever you are asked. The interview will take place either in a Conference Room, at a studio or in your own office. If it is in a studio your party will be so large – Press Officer, divisional official, Private Secretary – that you will give the impression that you have come to take over the place. This will be reinforced by the mass of documentation that the official will bring along, to which you will not refer but which will provide you with a feeling of security. If it is in your office this will mean an invasion by television crews, who will bring in cameras, cables, large metal boxes, lights and clapper boards and cause both upheaval and excitement, never hesitating to rearrange the furniture, pictures or ornaments to suit their refined visual sense.

It is in your office that you will also have your interviews with individual journalists. These will include specialist journalists writing for mass-circulation publications; specialist journalists writing for specialist journals (*The Concrete Mixer, Cybernetics*); foreign journalists, generally Americans, Germans or Scandinivians, writing in their respective languages; and foreign television interviewers, generally Swedes or Japanese. For most of these a Press Officer and your Private Secretary will be present. However, when seeing an extremely senior journalist or one very well known to you, you will want to speak to them alone. This, though, can lead to snags, since there will then not be a record of what has been said. And not only you but the journalists may need such a record. In these circumstances you should, if required, do your best to be helpful.

I shall always be grateful to Richard Crossman for – among so many other things – his considerateness to me when he was Minister of Housing and I was political correspondent of the *New Statesman*. I saw him one Monday evening and he gave me a good exclusive story, an advance outline of the contents of his new housing Bill. I took many notes and, as the evening wore on, a good deal of whisky as well. Next day, at my desk and with a headache to contend with, I opened my notebook and began to write my column. I was, however, unable to proceed, since what filled the pages of my notebook was not legible handwriting but what might have been either shorthand or Arabic, had I known how to write either. The editor would soon be asking for my column, and I was filled with despair. However, the telephone then rang. It was Crossman, who as an ex-*New Statesman* journalist also knew it was my copy day. 'Gerald,' he said, 'there are just a few details I would like to add to what I told you last night.' And he then gave me the whole story, in every particular, all over again. That, Minister, is how you should behave to journalists if you can.

There is one other kind of journalist who you hope will pay attention to you. This is the cartoonist. Cartoonists are even more idiosyncratic in their approach than the sketch writers. They will draw you how they see you, and you should be grateful that they draw you at all, however they see you, particularly if they do not have to put a label on you to identify you. Nicholas Garland, the greatest political cartoonist since the magnificent and lovable Vicky, drew me occasionally looking like a Japanese businessman. But who was I to complain?

Try never to complain – to cartoonists or to anyone else. Complaints will get you nowhere, and only make you look foolish. If a journalist writes about you in a particularly hostile way do not ring up his proprietor or send for a horse whip. Invite him round to your office for a drink. And never complain to one kind of journalist about another. The Lobby Correspondent is not responsible for the sketch writer, the leader writer, the gossip columnist, the headline writer or the cartoonist. He may not even have seen what they have written or drawn.

You will see and need the press both at home and away. When you travel within Britain on official business always hold a press conference and make yourself available to regional television and local radio. Remember that they see ministers less often than the London-based press and value them more. Take into account that regional newspapers are very widely read and trusted, that the early evening regional magazine programmes on television have big audiences among those who sensibly eat their main meal of the day at that time, and that local radio has great influence too. Just because you do not see these journalists regularly, do not undervalue them. And make sure you have a local angle for them. In Manchester, that queen of cities, the journalists are not a bit interested in Liverpool; and the people of Leeds regard Sheffield as an overdeveloped town in north Derbyshire. You will find that few fellow politicians will comment on your national television appearances but that provincial MPs will always have seen you on their regional screens.

When you travel abroad you will be preceded by your Central Office of Information Press kit. The same biographical details and repulsive photograph will crop up in Los Angeles, Helsinki and Hong Kong. In these places and others you will make more news than you expected. The number of British ministers visiting Seoul or Kansas City is not all that large. The journalists in these places will know little about your country, and you can help to put them right. Take trouble with them, and do not be put out if they behave differently from British journalists. Some of them may be too timid or overawed to put any questions to you, and these you will feel could well teach a lesson or two to their colleagues in London.

Take trouble, too, with British journalists based abroad. Indeed, take particular trouble with them, for they are far from home and feel they have the right to a good story from a visiting compatriot. They will not like it if you snub them. So always be ready to give private interviews to British journalists and to go out of your way to do so. For failing to do this in Brussels I was very rightly punished. I attended there a Common Market Ministerial Council on steel which should have finished the same evening as it started, but in fact hardly began. Instead of going home by a comfortable flight I had to stay overnight in an hotel horrible even by the standards of Brussels. The meeting then dragged on all the next day. When it finally faltered to its end I could not wait to get away from the place, and my Private Secretary had arranged a flight home for me that I was determined to get. Towards the end of the Council I was told that British journalists had asked for a briefing from me. By then I was so out of temper that I simply snarled a refusal, and raced away from the Council chamber to the airport as fast as I could.

I had acted stupidly. Brussels is a wasps' nest of news, and journalists from abroad specializing in European stories rely on their own ministers for an accurate briefing. My visit to Brussels was incomplete without my having given such a briefing. Even though I had entirely fulfilled my remit at the Council itself I had not properly carried out my mission for my government. A few days later I saw in the *Guardian* that I had been awarded the wooden spoon for my lack of co-operation with British journalists posted to the Common Market. I felt at the time that it was very unfair, but it was perfectly fair. The journalists had waited for the end of the meeting, just as much inconvenienced as I. The difference was that after the long wait they were still anxious to carry out their job and I was not. I never made this mistake again, and you should never make it at all.

To co-operate with a journalist or not is a decision you will make for yourself. You will do so taking account of his talents, his reliability and the newspaper for which he works. It is your right to refuse to talk to him, though he may afterwards find ways of penalizing you. If you do agree to talk to him, it is your duty to tell him the truth. A journalist to whom you have refused to speak will grumble about you, but will have no right to any other grudge against you. A journalist to whom you lie will never forget and will never trust you again. And remember, a minister is only as good as his last notice.

18

How to Reconcile Your Constituents

———

When you are appointed to the government you will get lots of letters of congratulations. Some will be from residents in your constituency. Your constituency political party will write too. They will be genuinely pleased that your qualities, which they recognized long ago, have been discerned by others. But they will also be uncertain, even worried. They will be concerned as to whether you are in danger of getting above yourself. Even those who like you best will be unable to stop themselves wondering: 'Will he get swollen headed and think he is too good for us now?'

Your constituency party is a group of politically sophisticated people. They will know that in accepting office you have surrendered a great deal of independence. They will be aware that, while as a back-bencher you devoted all your time to the constituency (or at any rate were expected to), now you will be distracted by other pressures. However loyal they may be to the government, they think for themselves politically and they will sometimes, perhaps often, disagree with government policies. They will understand that as a minister you will be unable to respond positively to their criticisms, except if you share them to the point of deciding to resign from the government. Some constituencies may feel that it brings them kudos to be represented by a minister. Others, on the contrary, will refuse to select as their candidate a person who is likely to be a minister, particularly if he makes it clear that it is his ambition to become one that motivates his desire to enter Parliament.

One safe Labour constituency, which had been represented by a Cabinet minister from 1964 to 1970, began looking for a new candidate after 1970 following the sitting Member's announcement that he would not contest the next election. It drew up the usual short list, and included in it a former Member of Parliament from another area. At the selection meeting this man was asked whether, if chosen as candidate, he would come to live in the constituency. He replied that he could not promise this, since he had hopes of ministerial office. He was passed over in favour of a local councillor. They had had enough of ministers in that constituency party.

Your constituents – those who write to you, who come to your advice bureaus, who simply read or hear about you – will wonder if you are going to neglect them now that you are in the government. They may not, in all their tens of thousands, have had much to do with you personally. But they still like to think that you are theirs if they need you. They do not much welcome the idea of your hobnobbing with civil servants in the fleshpots of London, a place of which in any case they are properly suspicious. One young MP, representing an apparently safe seat, was appointed to junior office in the Labour government of 1974 and promptly told his constituents that they could not expect to see so much of him now that he was a minister. They decided to see nothing at all of him, and in the 1979 general election entirely eliminated his large majority.

You cannot expect your constituents to be aware of all the technicalities with which you have to contend: your inability any longer to raise constituency matters in debate, to ask questions, even to sign harmless parliamentary motions. If, though, they write to you to complain of government policies, or to ask you to vote against the government on some matter that concerns them, they will discover that as long as you are a member of the government you are bound hand and foot to whatever it does. You will be even less independent than the most loyal government back-bencher since even he will occasionally rebel for constituency reasons and be forgiven for it, while you can never rebel at all and remain in the government. Indeed, far from publicly dissociating yourself from the government, you will be bound to defend it even when you disagree with it.

You are therefore in a delicate position. You can of course seek to resolve it by putting your government position first and your constituency nowhere. This, apart from being poor thanks to those who have selected you, canvassed for you and voted for you, will be an act of self-destruction. As Stanley Clinton Davis – himself for five years a junior minister while remaining an active constituency MP – put it, compellingly: you can be an MP without being a minister but you cannot be a minister without being an MP. If you are a minister, you must work harder in your constituency than you did before you were a minister. It can be done if you try; all you have to do without is sleep.

There you are, then, in your brand new tower block in Victoria Street or listed building in Whitehall. The distance between that rarefied existence and your constituency is not simply one of miles or hours; and you have to bridge that distance. It is therefore essential that you should not be cut off from the outside world by your ministerial preoccupations. Your Private Office will take care to protect you even when you have no wish for protection: partly because you are less trouble to them if they have you under their control, partly to safeguard you from cranks and eccentrics. You should therefore take care in your very first hour in your department to explain to your Private Office that you have a constituency and that it is very important to you. After all, otherwise how are they to know? Constituencies to them are vague troublesome places to which ministers keep having to go. You can make the point pretty bluntly, as I did, and explain that you knew your constituency long before you came to your department and hope to go on knowing it long after you leave the department.

One way of getting a bad reputation in your constituency pretty quickly after attaining ministerial office is to be persistently unavailable on the telephone. If people used to contacting you at the House of Commons are unable to get through to you after several attempts, they will give up trying and think the worse of you. They will not know, and if they get to know will be far angrier, that you were not even aware that they had telephoned because your Private Office did not tell you. You should therefore eliminate all chance of this happening by instructing your Private Office that your constituency officers and agent must be put through to you automatically, and that no one who telephones claiming to be a constituent should be turned away, at any rate until you have been consulted. This is particularly important if you do not have a constituency secretary working at Westminster to deal with your parliamentary commitments. The very efficient House of Commons telephone switchboard is likely to put all calls for you through to your office in the department rather than take messages as they do for back-benchers.

You will also want to make sure that your Private Office sets aside time in your daily diary for your constituency work. Everyone will have their own arrangement. Mine was without fail to reserve an hour every day with my constituency secretary to deal with correspondence and to build the rest of my ministerial day round this session. Of course, the time had to be changed if I had Cabinet Committees or parliamentary commitments. However, to establish the rule is important, even if it has to be varied. When Harold Wilson was Prime Minister, a regular period every afternoon between Tuesday and Thursday was kept for his constituency and political work. Only a major crisis was allowed to alter that fixture.

Your relationship with your constituency party must be founded on honesty. If they are critical of the government it is useless to pretend to them that you think they are right and the government wrong. If you adopt this attitude consistently, far from welcoming it they will think you are pretty hypocritical to remain in the government if you disagree with it so much. You will be respected far more if you explain and defend the government's position. Your constituency colleagues should in any case know you well enough to understand your underlying convictions. It will interest them as politicians to hear the government's case put with knowledge and experience even if they reject it. You may even convince them; and hearing the case will give them ammunition with which to defend the government to others. Do not, however, regard yourself simply as an ambassador from the government to the constituency. You can take messages back from your constituency to the government, and the government will profit from the exchange. After all, this information is at least as authentic as the news you and your colleagues get from civil servants and the press.

Of course membership of the government does not exclude you from constituency political activities. You will continue to report regularly to your party from Parliament. And you can, for example, take part in party fund-raising events. When my constituency party organized a sponsored march round the divisional boundaries I managed to get the entire Cabinet to sponsor me; some of them even paid up. You can, in addition, canvass for your council candidates in local elections and help to get voters to the poll on election day. One uncovenanted gain from this will be that not only your party members but also your constituents get the chance to see you, assuming, of course, that this is an experience they find acceptable.

It is, indeed, more important than ever before that you are seen in your constituency, in the streets and shops and schools and clubs and pubs. You should make a point of carrying out constituency engagements even more frequently than when you were a back-bencher. And you should never, unless an emergency of the first rank arises, cancel constituency engagements in favour of minis-terial commitments. During the crisis threatening the future of Chrysler UK at the end of 1975, sudden visits to London by various persons from Detroit – whose names (and sometimes behaviour) caused them to appear to be members of the Mafia – made urgent week-end meetings in London necessary. When the first of these unexpected events occurred, one Cabinet minister who had to cancel a constituency engagement regarded this as a disaster, while another similarly placed welcomed it as a blessed relief. If you adopt the attitude of the second of these, you should not be an MP, let alone a minister. Neglecting your constituency can become a bad habit. I remembered this when I was asked by my department, one Friday morning, to fly to Paris that same day to discuss aircraft problems with my French ministerial counterpart. I already had an engagement that evening in a local primary school in Manchester to discuss children's play facilities, and I spent Friday evening in the primary school, not in Paris, which I like to think was able to get along without me better than the primary school. Of course, in such situations you need to make a judgment about priorities, and sometimes Paris will have to come first. What is important is that Paris should not automatically come first.

As a minister you will, as we have seen, get national press and television coverage quite easily. Your constituents will read (or at any rate get the opportunity to read) about these activities with mild interest and possibly even with pleasure. They will not, however, regard it all as having very much to do with them. They will in particular not be likely to be favourably impressed by your travels abroad to exotic places at their expense when many of them have difficulty in getting farther than the Lake District on a coach trip. On the other hand they will be very interested in what you do in your own constituency, in streets and areas that they know and on issues that matter to them. You can leave your own department's press department to look after your national publicity. You should look after your constituency publicity yourself, taking care to ensure that your local newspapers, radio and television cover your activities as a local representative. Any minister can travel to far-away places. Not every minister is photographed and televised leading a children's march to demand better playgrounds.

Every MP likes to be thought a good constituency MP. You will, if you are sensible, seek to achieve something even more difficult, namely, to ensure that your constituents do not resent your membership of the government. You will discover in addition that your constituency work can make you a better minister too. His constituency is a Member of Parliament's university; it teaches him about basic problems in a way that political theory, however soundly based, never can. It can also help him to understand the impact on communities and individuals of the policies he pursues as a minister. If you are lucky your constituency work may even overlap with your departmental work; never be diffident if it does. I was, when I attended a Cabinet Committee which was discussing an issue on which I had a strong constituency interest. The Prime Minister, James Callaghan, was chairman of the Committee and called on me to speak for my department. I began by declaring my constituency interest, and cautiously asked whether it disqualified me from putting my case. James Callaghan retorted that my constituency interest particularly qualified me to speak. I then proceeded and, by no means due to my own advocacy, my side won. I never again hesitated to draw on my constituency experience in governmental discussions.

This did not, of course, mean that I invariably acted single-mindedly on behalf of my own area. When the National Enterprise Board was established, the government decided that it should have regional offices in the North-West and the North-East. Lord Ryder, then the chairman, wanted to establish the North-Western office in Manchester. It would have been easy for me to agree and then go to Manchester and claim the credit. However, I felt that Liverpool, with far worse employment problems, had the greater claim and I insisted that the office went there. On the other hand, when British Shipbuilders wanted to site their headquarters in Liverpool, I pressed very hard that it should go to Newcastle instead, believing that Newcastle's far greater shipbuilding interest gave it a better claim than the county where my own constituency was situated. Altruism is not only good for the soul, it gives you a clear conscience to fight for your own constituency when it really counts. Of course as a minister you are well placed to fight for your constituency in other ways. You can trade off favours with colleagues, paying official visits to their constituencies on matters important to them in exchange for a special favour in return.

Your constituents will be interested to have seen you on television on Thursday night if they meet you in their local club on Friday night. They will tolerate the more exotic and – to them – unattainable aspects of your ministerial life provided that you do not flaunt them. After my appearance in Washington for the Coleman hearings on Concorde I returned to my constituency for a tenants' association meeting in a particularly run-down block of flats. The woman who was the main energizing force in this association was one of those tough Northern ladies who make a definite point of taking no nonsense from anyone. As we sat around in her flat drinking tea and getting ready to discuss vandalism in the lifts and flooding on the verandas, she gave me an appraising look and accusingly remarked: 'I saw you on television gallivanting about in America.' Then she paused and added, more accommodatingly: 'Still, I've got to say it, we do see you here.' I could have asked for no greater accolade.

There are two ways in which you will be able to tell that you have been able to reconcile your constituents to your being a minister. You can regard it as a genuine compliment if they make it clear that they think of you not as a minister but as their own Member of Parliament. The real test, though, will be when you lose office. With luck, and provided you have conducted yourself with prudence and good sense, your constituents will accept you back with a warmth that shows that as far as they are concerned it did not matter whether you were a minister or not. And when you do lose office you will realize that it was your constituency that kept you sane and helped you to retain a sense of proportion as you rode about with your red box in your government car.

19

How to Leave Office Gracefully

(or, anyhow, as gracefully as possible)

––––––

Sooner or later you will stop being a minister. There are various ways of doing this.

The most dramatic and personally satisfying is to resign. Now of course you can resign through ill-health; or feel it necessary to resign through involvement in a scandal; or give up government office in order to become chairman of one of the remaining nationalized industries or similar body. However, the most potentially creditable reason for resigning is on an issue of principle. Even a resignation of this kind can, though, easily be forgotten. However, if handled properly it may be remembered for many years and even employed to your eventual advantage.

The first rule is simple but absolutely basic. If you are contemplating resigning your ministerial office, be entirely sure that you want to go. Because, unless you are so important or potentially disruptive that the Prime Minister may wish to try arguing you out of it, there will be no turning back once your letter of resignation has arrived at Number Ten. During one of Harold Wilson's premierships a junior minister, Norman Buchan, resigned from the post he held because he found it difficult to work with the ministerial head of his department. He had somehow got it into his head that he could give up this particular post while remaining a member of the government, at large, as one might say, and was considerably put out to learn that he was no longer a minister of any kind. However, this realization came too late. The only way, after committing this grievous error, that he could make himself felt was by causing trouble about moving out of his ministerial room at the House of Commons; and this he proceeded to do, eventually disappearing down the corridor in a cloud of grumbles.

If you are really perfectly certain that you do want to go, then make sure that you go on the right issue. If you choose one which has some meaning for your party or in the country, you will make an impact at any rate of some kind, short- or long-lasting. If you resign for a reason which makes little sense to many people, you will depart to a reaction of indifference or even derision. Everyone interested in politics remembers that Aneurin Bevan, Harold Wilson and John Freeman resigned from Clement Attlee's government in 1951 because they challenged the assumptions behind Hugh Gaitskell's Budget; that the Treasury team headed by Peter Thorneycroft (and including Enoch Powell) resigned from Harold Macmillan's government in 1958 due to disagreements over public expenditure. Enoch Powell, it is worth recalling, made something of a habit, even a career, out of resignation or its equivalent. He joined Thorneycroft and Nigel Birch in leaving Macmillan's government; together with Iain Macleod he refused to serve in Sir Alec Douglas-Home's Cabinet in 1963; was removed from Edward Heath's Shadow Cabinet in 1968 following his 'rivers of blood' speech about immigration; and removed himself from Parliament for several months (and from the Conservative Party permanently) in 1974 in protest at Edward Heath calling a general election. This might be said to be going for overkill; but it was overkill with finesse, since the reason for each resignation is still easily recalled.

At junior level, too, it is possible to depart accompanied by some *réclame*, as was achieved by Sir Edward Boyle's departure from Sir Anthony Eden's government in 1956 in protest at the Suez invasion; Edward Taylor's resignation from Edward Heath's government in 1971 when he found himself unable to concur with that government's wish to enter the Common Market; and Robert Cryer's decision to give up office in James Callaghan's administration in 1978 following that government's inability, after a series of rescues, to salvage the Kirby co-operative yet one more time.

However, if you choose an issue that does not make clear sense to fellow politicians or the press then you may have resigned in vain, assuming that you wish some potential change (other than your own departure) to be consequent upon your resignation. When Ray Gunter resigned as Minister of Power from Harold Wilson's government in 1968, no one was quite clear why he had done so, though there was a vague feeling that it was due to the rather muddled moves then going on for the kind of 'government of

national unity' that is regularly proposed during a Labour government's period of office but never when the Conservatives are in
power. Some cruel observers felt that, whatever reason he offered,
he had really gone because the job was too hard for him, what with
all those figures and pieces of paper. As Minister of Labour, a post
he held successfully, he was able to get along with considerable
accomplishment on the basis of having drinks with people at the
Marquis of Granby and elsewhere. When Gunter resigned and
returned, as he put it, to 'the folk from whence I came', he himself
commented with some modesty that he would be forgotten within
ten years. The reason for his resignation, if it was ever understood
or remembered at all, faded, sadly, much more quickly than that.

George Brown's resignation in 1968 was a classic example of a
politician resigning on the wrong issue. Brown was an exceptionally effective minister in the Labour government, full of energy and
drive, and immensely popular on public platforms. As Secretary of
State for Economic Affairs he advocated a policy of economic
growth. When this had to be abandoned at the time of the sterling
crisis in July 1966, Brown considered resignation so publicly that it
became almost a form of *cinéma vérité*, with television interviews
on the doorstep of Number Ten. If he had gone then he would have
been supported by a large following in both the Parliamentary
Labour Party and the country, which believed in growth
accompanied by devaluation of the pound rather than the stringent
measures which Harold Wilson and James Callaghan reluctantly
felt they had to adopt. However, he decided to stay after all, and
was appointed Foreign Secretary. Two years later he resigned for a
reason which just did not make sense to most students of politics.
Yet another economic crisis had broken out and the measures
adopted to deal with it called for a bank holiday, for which an
emergency Privy Council had to be summoned at Buckingham
Palace. At the necessarily very short notice George Brown could not
be found, and the Council was held without him. He felt that he
had been deliberately omitted, and next day from the Foreign
Office across the road sent in a letter of resignation.

In all the time I worked for Harold Wilson I only saw him
dejected on two occasions. The first, quite inexplicably to me, was
when the Liberals gained Birmingham Ladywood from Labour in a
by-election in 1969. By-elections in those days were depressing

events. The government was deeply unpopular and, when even safe seats fell vacant, the Conservatives gained them more often than not. Wilson, a glutton for punishment, would watch the television coverage of the by-election declaration in his study at Number Ten. Marcia Williams and I would join him, a little party in vigil at a political sick-bed. Somehow it was all made more gruesome by the BBC's habit of televising Spanish lessons late on Thursday nights, through whose demented and incomprehensible conversations and situations we would have to sit while waiting for the latest instalment of bad news. Even so, Wilson would endure the whole experience while retaining his characteristic perkiness. This, however, totally deserted him for the Ladywood result and he fell into a deep gloom for a while. It was ironic that the following year, at a general election which temporarily ended Wilson's premiership, Ladywood was comfortably regained while some of the other lost seats were not.

When George Brown's letter of resignation arrived in Downing Street in March 1968 it plunged Wilson into a depression much greater by far than the defeat at Ladywood. His five-year partnership with Brown, ever since they had raised their joined hands at the Labour Party Conference in Scarborough in 1963, was about to come to a finish; it was almost as if a marriage was ending. For this time Wilson saw that the resignation would go through. Telephone messages from Brown's Parliamentary Private Secretary, Ernest Davies, came in during the afternoon; Davies was anxious to see if a way could be found for Brown to stay. Wilson was that day marooned in one of the state rooms on the first floor sitting for his portrait, which Ruskin Spear was painting. I carried the messages to him as they came, but Wilson knew it was no good; this time Brown was going to go. When Brown did go, Labour MPs were perplexed. And his resignation statement in the House of Commons did not solve their puzzlement.

A resignation statement from the back benches is one of the traditional methods for an ex-Cabinet minister to explain his reasons for leaving the government. It is, indeed, very important for a minister who resigns to make clear the cause of his going, and to handle his departure with skill. After this his access to the news media will be severely limited, but at that moment he has almost the freedom of the air and the press. If you are senior enough to qualify for a resignation statement, take great care with it. The House will be more crowded than for any other speech you have made. Your own side will be interested: ready to be sympathetic, equally prepared to be critical. The Opposition will naturally be hoping to make political capital out of a government split. The House of Commons being an exceptionally difficult and fickle audience, you must draft your statement so that you get it absolutely right. In 1951 Aneurin Bevan decidedly did not, while Harold Wilson equally definitely did. Indeed, the credit he built up from his resignation, particularly with left-wing MPs, was decisive in his being elected to the party leadership twelve years later.

One notably successful resignation statement was that of Frank Cousins, who resigned, as Minister of Technology, in July 1966 at the time that George Brown did not. Cousins had entered Parliament in 1965 when already a minister, straight from the General Secretaryship of the Transport and General Workers' Union. He was painfully unhappy in the House of Commons, and embarrassingly clumsy when speaking from the Dispatch Box. Freed from office and speaking from the traditional third bench below the gangway, he was fluent, convincing and patently sincere. He resigned from Parliament the following year, with great relief, just at the time when he was getting good at being an MP. In melodramatic contrast to Cousins' elegiac farewell was the savage resignation speech of Sir Geoffrey Howe – oratory as a blood sport – in 1990. In despatching Margaret Thatcher to the political knackers' yard, Sir Geoffrey's ministerial quietus demonstrated that death really does have its sting.

Another optional tradition of an important ministerial resignation is an exchange of letters. These, both from the outgoing minister and the Prime Minister, will generally contain so many effusions of mutual personal esteem together with assurances of continuing support for the government from the new back-bencher that it will be difficult to understand why he has actually decided to fracture this moving friendship. Remember, however, when you leave the government you may swamp radio and television (and earn yourself a few useful fees to make up for the hefty drop in salary); but it is the Prime Minister who will have the last word. He, after all, has the Downing Street press machine at his disposal, and his every action is in any case being followed avidly by other

Members of Parliament decently prepared to help him out by taking on the job you have vacated. One junior minister who resigned during James Callaghan's premiership was awarded a farewell interview, at which he asked the Prime Minister whether there would be an exchange of letters. Callaghan dismissively replied that that would not be necessary though, if the now ex-minister had any keys or anything of that description, they should be handed in. Even that was not his final riposte. He appointed no one else to fill the vacated position, making it clear that the remaining ministers in the department could easily cope with the small amount of additional work involved.

If you are possessed of some political flair, you may arrange not simply to resign but to get yourself dismissed. This was the method chosen by Eric Heffer in April 1975, when he decided that Harold Wilson's dispensation for ministers to oppose government policy in the Common Market referendum campaign outside Parliament was not enough; he wanted to debate against his ministerial colleagues in Parliament as well. Heffer therefore created an interesting precedent by, as a minister, speaking from the back benches against the government of which he was still a member. This was, as he expected and intended, noted, and his membership of the government brought swiftly to an end. He subsequently, as we have seen, waltzed comfortably on to the Labour Party National Executive and almost everyone was therefore made cheerful, not excluding Gregor MacKenzie who shortly after was happily appointed to fulfil capably the duties Heffer had equally contentedly abandoned.

If you resign, either explicitly or (as in Eric Heffer's case) constructively, you have the right to dissociate yourself from the actions of the government you have left. After all, you have shown at some sacrifice to yourself what you thought of these actions and everyone knows where you stand. What will meet with less sympathy is if you decide to stay and then, when the whole government goes out of office, seek to convey to those interested that you disapproved of a great deal that was done while you were a member of the government that was doing it. Following the Labour government's defeat in the 1979 election two former junior ministers attempted this course of action at the subsequent Labour Party Conference. This pair were greeted with derision, not least by those they were attempting to please. Delegates wanted to know, with justice, why these two men of principle had found it possible to remain in the government – steeling themselves to accept its salary and perquisites – if they felt it to be so misguided or wrong-headed.

Getting yourself sacked voluntarily is one thing; being dismissed when you are ready, even anxious, to stay is quite another. Harold Wilson, being a soft-hearted man, used to dread the reshuffles he periodically carried out as Prime Minister. If the dismissed minister did not cut up too rough, Wilson would say afterwards, with intense relief: 'He took it like a gentleman.' However, Wilson disliked reshuffles nowhere nearly as much as those with whom he so reluctantly parted. In a sense it is more comforting to be dismissed with many others, since that way you feel it is not just you, just as electoral defeat can be borne a little more equably if you are not alone in humiliation. When at the counting of votes in Gillingham, where I was candidate in 1959, I found that instead of reducing the Conservatives' 4,000 majority I was being defeated by some 7,000, I wondered whether there was something about me that my best friends had not told me. Then the news was brought in that Arthur Bottomley, the immensely popular MP for neighbouring Rochester and Chatham, who had made a habit of holding his seat against national swings for a decade, had this time lost it with an adverse swing almost as big as the one against me. I was naturally far more distressed by his painful defeat than by my own modest lack of success; but I understood then that I was the victim of a national trend rather than a personal vendetta.

In the same way, a minister sacked in a mass government purge at any rate finds comfort in numbers. Such, presumably, were the feelings of the six members of Harold Macmillan's Cabinet who were summarily dismissed in July 1962. Harold Wilson thereafter regularly referred to this event, with political licence, as the time that Macmillan had sacked half his Cabinet: 'the wrong half, as it turned out'. These men, bruised as they undoubtedly felt, were not however visited with the humiliation of John Parker, a junior minister who was removed from office early in Clement Attlee's period as Prime Minister and who, when he diffidently asked the Prime Minister why he had been dismissed, received the brusque reply: 'Not up to the job.'

If you are sacked, you should decide with some care how you will react and from then on conduct yourself accordingly. During

Harold Wilson's first government, William Ross, the Secretary of State for Scotland, convinced himself that he was marked out for dismissal and assured friends that, if this happened, he would accept it amicably, and indeed with gratitude for the period of office he had been allowed to have. In fact, Wilson never removed him. On the one occasion when he might have contemplated doing so, any such thought was displaced from his mind by a tumultuous welcome for Ross which he witnessed when attending a Scottish Labour Party Conference.

You may decide, as Ross did, to take dismissal well. You may well react to it apathetically, sinking even deeper into the lethargy that possibly caused your removal. You may decide to bide your time, hoping for a change of heart from the Prime Minister who sacked you or for better luck from a successor. This can work out very well. Geoffrey Lloyd, a member of Churchill's 1951 Cabinet, was sacked in 1955 when Sir Anthony Eden became Prime Minister. Lloyd expected this since he had never got on with Eden. However, in 1957 Eden went, Harold Macmillan took over, and Lloyd returned to the Cabinet. He only lasted a couple of years, but at least he had had another turn. Judith Hart had similar luck twenty years later. She left Harold Wilson's government in 1975, refusing to accept what she regarded as demotion; in 1977, James Callaghan meanwhile having become Prime Minister, she returned to office in precisely the same post of Minister of Overseas Development that she had held two years before. Meanwhile she played an active part both in Parliament and on the National Executive Committee of the Labour Party, where the potential support of her vote was presumably not unwelcome to Callaghan when he reappointed her to office.

Work in your party can, indeed, be a road back to office. Selwyn Lloyd, following his dismissal as Chancellor of the Exchequer in Macmillan's 1962 July purge ('Selwyn Lloyd ausgebootet', moaned a German-language newspaper which gave me my first news of this dramatic event) accepted an assignment to conduct a survey of the Conservative Party's organization. Lloyd returned to office in 1963 as Leader of the House of Commons in Sir Alec Douglas-Home's administration, eventually ending a rich Commons career as the Speaker. He then went to the House of Lords, another avenue open to you upon dismissal, provided that you are of sufficiently senior rank and do not find consignment to this political depository too distasteful.

You may decide to be vengeful and work for the ousting of the Prime Minister who ousted you, in the hope that you will earn sufficient credit with his successor to get back to office. Several of those dismissed or passed over by Edward Heath when he was Prime Minister adopted this course, and were rewarded first by the humiliation of their foe and then by the award of a ministerial post by his grateful successor. If you decide that this, rather than turning the other cheek, is the way forward for you, you would be well advised to be a sincere Conservative. That party efficiently dispatched eight discarded Prime Ministers between 1935 and 1990, whereas the Labour Party has either acclaimed or at any rate put up with all three of its ex-Prime Ministers, though of course from time to time grumbling about them in the way that the Labour Party tends to do.

On the other hand, you may give up all expectation of office and busy yourself with other parliamentary activities. The House of Commons, in its accommodating way, is prepared to find a niche for anyone who needs one. There are chairmanships (or at any rate memberships) of Select Committees, places on the panel of Standing Committee chairmen, chairmanships of Party Groups, and numerous other posts which are both absorbing and prestigious. You may, however, come to the conclusion that you have had enough of it all, and leave political life altogether. Following his dismissal from Harold Wilson's Cabinet in 1969 Richard Marsh was appointed front-bench spokesman on housing when the Labour Party returned to Opposition the following year, but was more attracted by a subsequent offer from the Conservative government of the chairmanship of British Rail, and eventually found himself among the vocal admirers of Margaret Thatcher.

Of course, the least humiliating way of leaving office is 'one out all out' – defeat of your government in a general election. You then have the relief of knowing that you had no personal responsibility for your ejection from your department, apart naturally from any special incompetence of your own which contributed to your party being hurled from power. Everyone will prepare themselves for this eventuality in their own way. When in April 1979 I left the Department of Industry in Victoria Street to travel to my constituency for the election campaign, I had already removed the few personal possessions I kept there, and had also completely emptied my ministerial room at the House of Commons. It was not that I particularly anticipated defeat; indeed, I was rather optimistic. However, I wanted in case of defeat to make a clean, clear break. Following the change of government I never once contacted my old department on official business. I had said my farewells to my Private Office three weeks before; after the election some of my former civil servants wrote kind letters to me and I replied. I returned my office pass and the keys to my red boxes by post. And, unlike the days of my superstitious refusal to go near Downing Street, I was able to walk past my old department – on my way to Boots the chemists or Baskin-Robbins' 31 ice-cream flavours – without a qualm.

Or at any rate, without much of a qualm; for you will find that there are withdrawal symptoms. After five years of pampered travel in a ministerial car you have to get used to using public transport in company with your fellow citizens again, and to the amazingly high fares that London taxi drivers are now charging. And you will have a much lower salary with which to pay those fares. The red boxes stop coming, leaving huge gaps to fill in your evenings. Instead of a comfortable department in which you could work – or take a nap – you have to scramble with your fellow former ministers and other Members of Parliament for the exiguous and constricted accommodation available in the Palace of Westminster or its outlying buildings, which of course back-benchers had to put up with – if they were lucky – during the five years when you were luxuriating in Marsham Street or Victoria Street.

Gone is your Private Office staff who had at the press of a buzzer made available to you all the resources of a great department of state. You are dependent on the goodwill of your constituency secretary – in my case, happily, readily volunteered even without being requested – for assistance with filing material, arranging of travel, research and typing of speeches, in addition to the huge constituency work load which may have helped you (to the intolerable nourishment of your vanity) to increase your majority in the election.

In the Commons Chamber itself you will feel disoriented. If you go on to the back benches you will, after all that time in government when you simply rose to speak whenever you wanted to, share again your colleagues' agonies of waiting to catch the Speaker's eye. If you are given duties on the front bench, you will feel that the Chamber is somehow facing the wrong way and that it should be swivelled round until you are sitting where you belong to the right of the Speaker's chair.

There will be the terrible moment when the minister who has replaced you rises to speak on the subjects you have made your own. It will be bad if he performs less well than you used to, intolerable if he is better. To his left and to his rear in the civil servants' box will be sitting not only the officials who used to brief you but even the very Private Secretary whom you yourself appointed. When you walk through Palace Yard you will see flashing through it the car in which you used to ride with the driver who used to drive you.

Gradually, though, you will get used to the change. You will no longer flinch when you see yourself described in the newspapers as an 'ex-minister'. The empty hours will fill with new activities. You will find a role in the House of Commons, and begin to be active and busy, sometimes even impossibly busy; though the outcome of your activities will be less definite than the consequences of the decisions you made as a minister. In your constituency you will be able to unite with the whole of your constituency party in opposing and campaigning against the policies of the government. Eventually you will begin to enjoy life in Opposition, though there will be occasional pangs of nostalgia. You will have to watch your own conversation and stop yourself beginning too many sentences with the words, 'When I was . . .' As the months go by you will find that the minister who replaced you, instead of being an ignorant tiro, now intolerably knows more about your beloved old responsibilities than you do.

You will have learned a lot. You will know when a minister is making his own speech or when he is just reading from a brief. You will be able to judge, from the replies ministers make, whether there has been a row in the Cabinet or a disagreement in the department, and you will be able to exploit this knowledge. You may even be able to guess on whose advice a minister is acting. After ministerial experience of defensive tactics in standing committees you will know how to provoke your counterpart into the kind of indiscretion or error which you learned to avoid – until the time comes when he has learned too. You will anticipate from the minister the procedural devices you used to employ, and act to counter or prevent them. You will know what questions to table, because you will know how the answers are drafted. And, because the minister knows you know, he will be very wary of you.

When you return to Opposition after a period in office you will not be the same person as the new back-bencher who enjoyed Opposition in his first Parliament. You will understand the kinds of Opposition activity that are useful and likely to produce results, and those which are just frustrating and pointlessly tiring. All-night sittings will not contain for you the spice they offered when you first entered Parliament. You will not be the same person to yourself; you will not be the same to others, either. You will be somewhat surprised to find that your colleagues regard you not only as a fellow Member but as an ex-minister. Newly elected members of the opposite party and even of your own may treat you with a certain respect. For although you have been deposed from your privileged position – and that may cause them, since they are only human, at any rate a little satisfaction – you have enjoyed experiences which by their very nature are denied to most people.

You have, after all, been a Minister of the Crown. You have attended Privy Councils and watched the pricking of sheriffs. Somewhere stowed away you have put the souvenir red box to which every former minister is entitled; although, for security reasons, the lock must be changed. As the Parliament proceeds and the government becomes unpopular, as all governments do at any rate for a time, you will begin to dare to hope that perhaps before too long you may become a minister again. Meanwhile, you will mull over your experiences in your mind. And it may be that the time will come when you hold some innocent, unwary and quite likely unwilling passer-by with your glittering eye and, before he can make an excuse and leave, begin to tell him how to be a minister.

Index
